Ashia's
Table

To my mom, Zarina

Ashia's Table

Family Recipes from India & beyond

Ashia Ismail-Singer

Photography by Manja Wachsmuth

Interlink Books

An imprint of Interlink Publishing Group, Inc.
Northampton, Massachusetts

First published in 2022 by
INTERLINK BOOKS
An imprint of Interlink Publishing Group, Inc.
46 Crosby Street
Northampton, Massachusetts 01060
www.interlinkbooks.com .

Text © Ashia Ismail-Singer, 2021
Design © Floor van Lierop, 2021
Food photography © Manja Wachsmuth, 2021
Location photography © unsplash.com, 2021
Family photographs from the private collection of
Ashia Ismail-Singer

Library of Congress Cataloging-in-Publication Data
available ISBN 978-1-62371-884-8

Printed and bound in Korea

Table of contents

Introduction

For the past eight years, I have been planning and writing this book. It is a culmination of my love of food and cooking, and of my wish to share my own, and my family's, recipes with others. Indian food does not have to be complicated. It can be easily made at home, with just a few basic ingredients. The recipes in this book have been created to be as simple as possible. I believe that anyone can learn to make a truly delicious Indian feast, or to bring a hint of Indian cooking to any healthy, nutritious, everyday meal.

Food evokes a passion in me that I cherish, one that has grown throughout my early childhood days in Malawi, Africa, my teenage years in England, and the last twenty-plus years in my beautiful adopted home country of New Zealand.

Being of Indian heritage, my love of cooking first started at early age, and some of my favorite recipes are ones that have been passed down through my family, adapted by each generation to suit the ingredients available. As a busy nurse, mother, and home cook, I have refashioned these recipes to reflect my own lifestyle and cooking techniques.

The Indian food that I make bears little resemblance to the Indian restaurant food that many Westerners eat, as takeout or dine-in. My home-cooked dishes are uncomplicated, require only a few key spices, and are fresh, healthy, and easy to prepare. Mine is an immigrant's cuisine of sorts, blending old traditions with new ones, creating food that spans generations, geography, and ethnicity.

My grandparents were Memon Muslims who came from Gujarat, on the western coast of India. Sometime in the late 1930s–early 1940s, they emigrated to Malawi, Africa. Memons originated in the northwestern part of ancient India, the Sindh region of modern-day Pakistan. The Memon language shares similar vocabulary with the Sindhi, Kutchi, and Gujarati languages, and also shares cultural similarities with the Khoja, Khatri, and Gujrati people. Memon lineage traces back to Lohanas of Sindh, and the origin of the name *Memon* comes from the word *mumin*, or "believer" in Arabic. The Memon community was founded in the fifteenth century when they converted to Islam.

Memons were predominantly merchant traders, of the Sunni Muslim sect. They were very business-minded and philanthropic, making sure that their community was well looked after. Due to their mercantile nature, they were never afraid to migrate and progress. Migration led Memons to Africa, to Asia, to the Americas and the Middle East. My grandparents left India to migrate to Africa, first to Mozambique, and then to Malawi to build a business and advance themselves.

My dad was born in India, in Jamnagar, in the southwestern part of Gujarat. He was only one year old when his family left to go to Malawi, known as the "warm heart of Africa." My mother's family were already in Malawi, and she was born there. My sisters and I were all also born in Malawi. Because of political instability, we left as a family in 1987 to emigrate to the UK. We all had British passports, since Malawi was part of the Commonwealth, and my father had lived and studied in the UK during the 1960s. It was a chance for a better life for us all.

Regardless of where we lived, cooking was always a big part of our upbringing. My parents loved to entertain, and my mom had no qualms about cooking a biryani, a layered meat and rice dish, for a hundred guests on special occasions. Together with my dad, they always planned what dishes were to be served at family gatherings.

We celebrated every festival and special family occasion with an abundance of food. My parents loved having parties for our birthdays, especially since my sister and I are twins. There weren't very many twins in Malawi in the 1970s, so we were a bit of a novelty! Religious festivities, like Eid, were always spent with the wider family and friends, and there would be meat and vegetarian dishes, my mom's famous biryani, the recipe for which is on page 82, and of course lots of amazing sweets, like jalebi (battered coils dipped in sugar syrup, page 189), burfi (sweet fudge with different flavorings, decorated with nuts, page 183), shortbread cookies with spices (page 184), and homemade kulfi (ice cream, page 198), with rose, cardamom, or mango.

I loved being in the kitchen with my mom, and with my aunts who would visit. Families always had an open door policy, so you never needed an invite. Our cook, Medson, prepared the ingredients, and then Mom would come in and finish things off. He would make excellent rotis (page 155); my mom taught him, too. I remember the fragrant smells of spices cooking, beautifully aromatic, heady, a mixture of hot, salty, sweet and sour, but perfectly balanced. Recipes were never written down but learned by taking part, helping and learning as you went, developing your tastebuds, which became more acute with age and experience.

In Malawi when I was growing up, fruit, vegetables, and meat did not come packaged. We grew our produce or slaughtered the animals ourselves. We had a chicken coup, which also housed goats. A couple of times a week before heading off to work, my dad would slaughter a chicken by slitting its throat and saying a prayer, making it halal. Then Medson would defeather and clean the chicken before it was presented as dinner. Goat was slaughtered the same way, but only every couple of months, and the meat was prepared and then frozen for later use. This was our normal and the way of life for me growing up in Africa. I have fond memories of me and my sisters and cousin going to the dairy farm with my mom and aunt to collect our milk, which we would carry home, sloshing about in a big aluminum milk pail.

The ingredients we used were always fresh, and the dishes were predominantly Indian. But Mom was making "fusion food" long before fusion was fashionable. Being a very confident cook, she effortlessly adapted Western recipes—Sunday roasts, casseroles, and shepherd's pie—to incorporate Indian flavors.

Moving to the UK from Malawi was a bit of a surprise for me. Although my father had lived in the UK in the 1960s, things had changed a lot when we emigrated there as a family in 1987. Before we emigrated, we had traveled as a family to the UK several times on vacation. But moving there as a teenager was a culture shock. Having lived a very sheltered lifestyle, it was quite confronting, coming across people who didn't accept you because you were different.

I navigated this new life with apprehension. But what brought me comfort and joy was being part of a very close-knit family and coming home from college and starting dinner.

Both my parents worked, and my sister and I, being the eldest of four girls, would come home and start cooking the family meal. I was studying fashion and design at art school, and I loved getting creative in the kitchen, too. It was here that my love of cooking blossomed. There was a large population of South Asians in the UK, so everything Indian was available, from spices to vegetables.

Moving to New Zealand on my own in 1997 was probably the most exciting—and also the hardest—thing I ever did. Always outspoken, and never one to follow what other girls in my community did, I followed my dream of wanderlust. I ended up here, falling in love not just with the country but with one Kiwi in particular, who I ended up marrying and having two amazing children with. Now, having spent more of my life in New Zealand than I did anywhere else, I truly call it home. But that doesn't stop me from being an immigrant and missing "home," which is ultimately wherever the rest of my family is, too.

Cooking Indian food really doesn't have to take hours. You can easily create a wonderful dinner or lunch using the simple recipes I have created. And as I say to everyone, it doesn't matter if you add a little more or less of one spice, or substitute a different protein, or use only vegetables if you want a meat-free meal. You can customize the recipes to suit your palate and family's eating style.

This book includes treasured recipes my mom taught me. And it's full of the ones I have created trying to recapture the flavors of my childhood here in New Zealand, so I can share them with my own children who are of mixed heritage, and leave a legacy for them. Every family—every person—has a story. Where they come from and where they end up is circumstantial. But, along the way, we all need food to sustain us. It nourishes life. It makes us who we are and creates memories that link us to our families and friends.

I have relished every minute of this journey, and I'm delighted to be sharing the recipes from *Ashia's Table* with you. I believe that food also celebrates life. So I hope that my easy-to-cook, simple, authentic, Eastern-inspired dishes feed your imagination to cook fabulous meals to share with your family and friends, ones that help create wonderful memories with those you love.

Much love,

Ashia

Pantry essentials

From the intense heat of chili to mellow garlic cloves, this section includes everything you will need to experiment with flavors and cook a beautiful Indian feast.

Pantry essentials

What I love about Indian cooking is that there are no rules. Every region has its own way of doing things and each family has its own culinary customs and traditions. My style of Indian cooking requires just a few core ingredients, and yet used in different combinations they create an array of different dishes that are simple to make and delicious to eat.

Onions

Onions are a staple ingredient for many of my recipes, fried until golden, or slightly darker for meat curries. As a child, when my mother was teaching me to cook, her first instruction was always "Get two onions and slice them up." It was a task I detested!

Garlic

Fresh garlic is best and I use it crushed or made into a paste. For convenience, you can use the ready-made variety. It is also available as a dried and ground seasoning.

Ginger

Again, fresh is best, either grated or as a paste, but it is also available pre-prepared.

Tomatoes

Tomatoes are another staple ingredient in my recipes. I use them in a variety of forms. While fresh tomatoes provide bulk to a recipe, I often find it easier to use canned or jarred tomatoes or tomato paste since there is little difference in taste and they last longer when stored.

Tamarind (Ambli/Imli)

A souring agent made from the pods of the tamarind tree, it can be bought as a pod with a husk and seeds, in a block of pulp or as a concentrate.

Cardamom (Elaichi)

The dried green pods of this plant are full of tiny brown/black seeds with a sweet flavor and pungent aroma. You can use the pods whole, adding them to your oil when cooking to start your base flavors, or extract the seeds inside the husk by crushing the pods under the flat of a knife.

Cinnamon sticks

This versatile spice is obtained from the rolled, dried bark of a tropical tree. It has a warm flavor and can be used in both sweet and savory dishes.

Cloves

These wonderfully aromatic flower buds are an excellent addition to meats and to add flavor to rice dishes such as biryani or pulau rice.

Crushed red pepper flakes

These are dried, coarsely ground chilies with seeds included. Typically hot, use them sparingly until you have an understanding of the amount of heat you prefer.

Cumin (Jeero)

The dried seed, from the flowering plant, has a slightly peppery flavor and can be used both ground and whole.

Coriander/Cilantro (Dhania)

The dried seeds of the cilantro or coriander plant have a spicy aroma and are an essential ingredient as a base of any Indian curry sauce. To intensify the flavor, dry-roast the seeds until aromatic and then crush them. I also use fresh cilantro as a garnish, or mixed with green chilies to make a paste (page 17).

Garam masala

Garam (hot) masala (spice mixture) is a traditional North Indian spice mix. To make your own:

2 tsp whole green cardamom pods
2 cinnamon sticks
2 tsp whole cumin seeds
1 tsp whole cloves
1 tsp whole black peppercorns

Remove the seeds from the cardamom and discard the pods. Heat a nonstick frying pan. Dry-fry the spices over low heat until the cumin turns golden brown. Remove from heat and grind to a fine powder. This will make 4 to 5 teaspoons. Store in an airtight container for up to six months.

Indian chili powder

Not to be confused with the spice mix labeled "chili powder" in many supermarkets, this is a richly flavored medium-hot ground chili used widely in Indian cuisine. You can find it in any South Asian grocery store, or substitute cayenne, but you may need to use a little less as cayenne has more heat.

Kashmiri chili (Mirch)

Made from dried, ground red chilies this is a vibrant mild–medium powder used for its intense color and heat.

Dhal

Dhal is a broad term that refers to a wide range of dried split lentils, peas, and beans, as well as the dishes you can create with them. They are nutritious and used in many Indian dishes. I usually have a variety of dhal in my pantry, including chana dhal (dried split chickpeas), mung dhal (dried split mung beans), as well as black and red lentils. Some require soaking overnight, while others can just be boiled from dry.

Mustard seeds

The tiny round seeds from the mustard plant have a nutty, peppery flavor and can be used whole or ground, often as a base flavor when you start heating the oil.

Paprika

This is made from dried ground sweet red peppers. I often use a combination of this and cayenne pepper in my cooking.

Turmeric (Hyder)

Part of the ginger family, this dried and ground spice provides a lovely yellow color to any curry dish. Turmeric has anti-inflammatory properties and is a powerful antioxidant. It can also be used fresh.

Saffron

Saffron strands are a deep orange color and have a musky aroma. Used in both sweet and savory recipes, a little goes a long way, which is good because it is the world's most expensive spice.

Green chili & cilantro paste

This is a very versatile paste and one of my mom's favorite ingredients, used to flavor a variety of dishes. It is best made fresh but you can make it in advance and store it in ice-cube trays in the freezer.

 Makes approx. 1 cup

large bunch of fresh cilantro
6–8 fresh green chilies

Wash the cilantro and dry well using paper towels or a clean tea towel. Remove the stalks of the cilantro, as these can give the paste a bitter aftertaste.

Roughly chop the chilies.

Blend the ingredients together with a handheld immersion blender or in a mortar and pestle.

If you are making the paste ahead, half-fill each compartment of an ice cube tray with ½–1 teaspoon of paste. Green chilies can vary in strength and heat, so only use a small amount until you establish the amount you like.

This keeps for up to one week in the refrigerator or for 3 months in the freezer.

Ghee (clarified butter)

Mom always used ghee as her main cooking fat when we were growing up. She had a large container of it sitting in the pantry. It's a beautiful golden color when heated and a luscious yellow when it cools.

 Makes approx. 1 cup

2¼ cups (500 g) unsalted butter

Melt the butter in a large heavy-based saucepan over low heat and continue to simmer until a thick foam appears on the surface of the butter.

Continue to simmer uncovered for 20–30 minutes until the milk solids settle at the bottom and the liquid is clear and golden. Watch closely because the milk solids at the bottom of the pan can burn quickly.

Meanwhile, line a sieve with a piece of cheesecloth and place the sieve over a bowl. Slowly pour the liquid through the cheesecloth, without disturbing the milk solids at the bottom of the pan. Discard the milk solids.

Leave the ghee to cool and then transfer it to a glass jar or container. Ghee will keep in the refrigerator for up to a year, or stored in a sealed jar at room temperature for up to 6 weeks.

Grazing & bites

These dishes are served as sharing platters when you are gathered with family and friends. From spicy samosas and little puris stuffed with shrimp and drizzled with tamarind, to the classic onion & potato bhajias, this is the street food of India right here in your kitchen.

Kebab pastry twists

These tasty pastry twists are great served as finger food at parties or as part of a sharing platter, accompanied with tamarind chutney (page 165) to give them a little extra bite.

❧ Makes 12–14　　　❧ Prep time: 30 mins　　　❧ Cooking time: 10 mins

10½ oz (300 g) ground lamb or beef
1 small onion, grated
1–2 garlic cloves, crushed
1 tsp grated fresh ginger
2 tsp green chili & cilantro paste
　(page 17)
½ tsp ground cumin
½ tsp salt
1 tbsp vegetable oil
2–3 sheets ready-rolled puff pastry,
　partially defrosted
1 egg, beaten, for egg wash

In a large bowl, combine the meat, onion, garlic, ginger, green chili & cilantro paste, cumin, and salt, then mix with a wooden spoon or with your hands until thoroughly combined. Divide the mixture into small sausage-like kebab shapes about 3 in (8 cm) long and 1 in (3 cm) in diameter.

Heat the oil in a shallow frying pan until hot, add the kebabs, and cook for approximately 6–8 minutes until browned on all sides. Keep turning the kebabs to ensure an even color.

Remove from the heat and transfer the kebabs to a plate lined with paper towels to drain excess oil. Set aside to cool.

Line a baking tray with foil. Prepare the pastry by cutting the sheets lengthways into ½ in (1 cm) wide strips. Wind one strip around a cooled kebab and place it on the prepared baking tray. Repeat until all the kebabs are enclosed in a pastry twist and then place the tray in the freezer for 15–20 minutes to set (or keep frozen for up to 3 months).

Preheat the oven to 450°F (230°C). Remove the tray from the freezer and brush the pastry with the beaten egg. Bake for about 10 minutes, or until pastry is golden and cooked through. Serve warm.

Spinach squares

This savory treat is one of my mother's recipes. It is packed full of great nutrients, so is perfect in a school lunchbox, but equally delicious served as an appetizer or finger food at a dinner party, with any sweet dipping sauce or apple chutney (page 162).

❤ Makes about 24   ❤ Prep time: 20 mins   ❤ Cooking time: 25–30 mins

10½–14 oz (300–400 g) spinach
¾ cup (90 g) gram (chickpea) flour
1 tsp baking powder
2 tbsp plain yogurt
3 tbsp canned chopped tomatoes
½ tsp salt
½–1 tsp Indian chili powder
  or cayenne
1 tsp ground coriander
½ tsp ground cumin
½ tsp ground turmeric
1–2 garlic cloves, crushed
1 egg
freshly ground black pepper
vegetable oil, for greasing

Preheat the oven to 300°F (150°C).

Wash the spinach and dry with paper towels or a clean tea towel. Trim any stalks off the spinach and discard, then finely chop the leaves.

Place the spinach in a large bowl and add the chickpea flour, baking powder, yogurt, tomatoes, salt, spices, garlic, and egg. Mix with a wooden spoon or with your hands until thoroughly combined.

Thoroughly grease a shallow 8 x 11 in (20 x 30 cm) baking dish with vegetable oil and line with parchment paper. Press the spinach mixture into the dish. It should be about ¾ in (2 cm) thick.

Bake for 25–30 minutes or until golden and set. Allow to cool before cutting into 2 in (5 cm) squares. Serve immediately, or shallow-fry in 3 tbsp vegetable oil for a crispy texture if desired.

Season to taste with freshly ground black pepper.

Onion & potato bhajias

A well-known Indian appetizer, these homemade bhajias are well worth the effort. They're great served hot as part of an Indian feast, but I love to have them cold the next day served with tamarillo chutney (page 165).

❤ Makes approx. 24   ❤ Prep time: 20 mins   ❤ Cooking time: 20 mins

generous ½ cup (60 g) gram (chickpea) flour
1 tsp salt
½ tsp ground cumin
1 tsp baking powder
½ cup (10 g) chopped cilantro
1 or 2 green chilies (optional), chopped
½–1 cup (120–240 ml) cold water
2 large potatoes
1 onion
vegetable oil, for deep-frying

In a large bowl, thoroughly combine the gram flour, salt, cumin, baking powder, cilantro, and green chilies (if using), then mix in the cold water using a wooden spoon until you have a thick batter consistency. Set aside.

Peel and grate the potatoes and thinly slice the onion. Add both to the batter and mix until well combined.

Pour the oil into a large pot to a depth of 2 in (5 cm). Heat until the surface shimmers and a small piece of bread turns golden. Working in batches, drop tablespoons of the bhajia mixture into the oil and fry for 6–8 minutes, turning from time to time, until golden and cooked through.

Using a slotted spoon, transfer the bhajias to a plate lined with paper towels to drain excess oil. Serve.

Ṭuna kebabs

These are easy to make and are great served on a platter, to take on picnics, or have as a light lunch with a fresh green salad. Serve with date and tomato chutney (page 163) and some cucumber raita (page 167).

❤ Makes approx. 14   ❤ Prep time: 20 mins   ❤ Cooking time: 20 mins

3 x 5 oz (140 g) cans chunky-style tuna in oil
5–6 potatoes, peeled, boiled, and mashed
½–1 tsp green chili & cilantro paste (page 17)
1 egg, beaten
breadcrumbs, for coating
vegetable oil, for frying
salt and freshly ground black pepper

In a large bowl, mix the tuna, mashed potatoes, green chili & cilantro paste, and season to taste with salt and pepper. Mix well with a wooden spoon or with your hands until thoroughly combined.

Divide the mixture into small sausage-like shapes approximately 3 in (8 cm) long and 1 in (3 cm) diameter.

Place the beaten egg and breadcrumbs in separate dishes. Dip the kebabs into the beaten egg and then coat with breadcrumbs.

Pour the oil into a large pot to a depth of 2 in (5 cm). Heat until the surface shimmers and a small piece of bread turns golden. Working in batches, fry the kebabs for 6–8 minutes, turning frequently, until evenly browned.

Using a slotted spoon, transfer the kebabs to a plate lined with paper towels to drain excess oil. Serve hot.

Samosas

Served as a snack in most Indian homes, my mom always has these gorgeous pastries in her freezer, ready to cook. If cooking from frozen, allow them to defrost in the refrigerator overnight. Deep-fried crispy samosas are typically a vegetarian dish, but I love this meat version as a delicious alternative.

❤ Makes 24   ❤ Prep time: 45 mins   ❤ Cooking time: 45 mins

pastry
2 cups (240 g) all-purpose flour,
   plus extra for dusting
½ tsp salt
2 tsp vegetable oil
approx. ¾ cup (180 ml) warm water

filling
1 tbsp vegetable oil
1 lb (500 g) ground lamb, chicken,
   or beef
½ tsp salt
1 tsp ground cumin
1 tsp ground coriander
1–2 garlic cloves, crushed
¼ tsp ground turmeric
¼ tsp freshly ground black pepper
¼ tsp garam masala
½–1 tsp Indian chili powder
   or cayenne (optional)
¼ cup (60 ml) tomato purée or
   passata
2 small onions, finely diced

assembly
¼ cup (30 g) all-purpose flour
2 tsp cold water (more if required)
vegetable oil, for frying

Sift the flour and salt into a large bowl. Make a well in the middle, pour in the oil and water, then mix and knead until a soft dough is formed. Cover the dough and set aside for 20 minutes to rest.

Once rested, divide the dough into 6 balls. On a floured surface, roll out each ball to a round about 9 in (23 cm) in diameter, basically as thin as you can get without tearing it. Heat a dry, nonstick frying pan over medium heat and brown the rounds lightly on both sides. The dough needs to be handled without breaking, so it is essential you do not overcook it. Repeat and place on a plate. Wrap with a damp tea towel until the filling is prepared.

In a large pot, heat the oil and add all the filling ingredients, except the onions. Cook, stirring occasionally, for 20 minutes. Add the onions and cook for a further 10 minutes until translucent and the mixture has no liquid. Set aside.

In a small bowl, mix the flour and water together to make a thick, spreadable paste. Cut the partially cooked pastry circles into quarters using a sharp knife. For each quarter, place a line of flour paste onto one of the straight edges and bring the opposite edge over, creating a cone shape. Fill the cone with filling mixture, then fold and paste the top edge over to make a tightly formed triangle.

Place the samosas on a tray and freeze for 30 minutes. If you are cooking them on the day, pour the oil into a large karahi (Indian wok) or frying pan to a depth of 2 in (5 cm). Heat until the surface shimmers and a small piece of bread turns golden. Reduce the heat to medium and add the samosas in batches. Fry, turning them from time to time, until golden brown.

Using a slotted spoon, transfer the samosas to a plate lined with paper towels to drain excess oil. Serve.

Pani puri with potato or shrimp filling

Everyone loves delicate crispy puris, which can be made at home (page 158) or bought pre-made from your local speciality store. Here are two wonderful savory filling suggestions (make them both to fill 20–25 puris), but the pastries are so versatile the possibilities are numerous. They are delicious with tamarind chutney (page 165).

❤ Makes 20–25   ❤ Prep time: 15–20 mins   ❤ Cooking time: 15–20 mins

potato filling
3–4 medium potatoes,
   peeled and finely cubed
¼ tsp turmeric
⅓ cup (50 g) cooked chickpeas
   (canned are fine)
salt

shrimp filling
½ tbsp vegetable oil
1–2 garlic cloves, crushed
10½ oz (300 g) cooked, peeled
   shrimp
¼ tsp salt
½ tsp Indian chili powder
   or cayenne
½ tbsp finely chopped cilantro

assembly
20–25 puri shells
tamarind chutney (page 165)
scant ½ cup (100 ml) plain yogurt
sev (fine Indian fried noodles),
   for sprinkling (optional)

For the potato filling: Boil the cubed potatoes in salted water with the turmeric until tender. Drain and leave to cool. Mix in the chickpeas.

For the shrimp filling: Heat the oil in a shallow frying pan until hot and cook the crushed garlic and shrimp for 2 minutes until the shrimp are warmed through. Add the salt and chili powder and cook for a further 2–3 minutes. Finally add the chopped cilantro, stir to combine, and then set aside to cool.

Assembly should only be completed just before serving so the puris remain crisp: Puris are very fragile, so carefully tap a ¾ in (2 cm) diameter hole in the top of each puri using the handle of a teaspoon. Fill each with a small spoonful of the potato or shrimp filling, a drizzle of tamarind chutney, and ½ tsp of the yogurt, and sprinkle the top with sev if you like.

Paneer & vegetable tikka

These tikka are made with a combination of soft, juicy paneer and chunky vegetables in a beautifully spicy sauce and then grilled to perfection. They are easy to make and sure to impress your family and friends at a summer barbecue. You can serve them with apple chutney (page 162) and yogurt.

❧ Makes 8–10   ❧ Prep time: 15 mins   ❧ Cooking time: 10 mins

10 wooden skewers, soaked in water
   for at least 5 minutes
apple chutney (page 162), to serve

marinade
1 tsp Indian chili powder
   or cayenne
1 tsp ground coriander
1 tsp ground cumin
½ tsp turmeric
1–2 garlic cloves, crushed
1 tbsp tomato paste
1–2 tbsp olive oil

tikka
10½ oz (300 g) paneer, cut into
   1 in (3 cm) cubes
4–6 large cremini mushrooms,
   cut into 1 in (3 cm) pieces
1 red bell pepper, cut into
   1 in (3 cm) pieces
1 green pepper, cut into
   1 in (3 cm) pieces

In a bowl, mix all the marinade ingredients together well and set aside.

Assemble each tikka by threading alternating pieces of paneer, mushroom, and red and green peppers, leaving a 2 in (5 cm) gap at each end for handling.

Lay the skewers on a tray lined with parchment paper and brush each one with the marinade, making sure all of the ingredients are well coated. Refrigerate for at least 30 minutes, but preferably 1–2 hours.

Cook on a hot grill or cast-iron griddle until cooked through and golden on all sides, 6–8 minutes. Serve with apple chutney.

Fish tikka

In India, tikka dishes are typically cooked in a clay oven called a tandoor, but I think this delicious dish works just as well on the grill or in a griddle pan, where you can still achieve the charred look of the tandoor.

❤ Makes 8–10   ❤ Prep time: 15 mins   ❤ Cooking time: 10 mins

10 wooden skewers, soaked in water
   for at least 30 minutes
mango chutney (page 163), or
   cilantro chutney (page 162),
   to serve

marinade
2 tbsp lemon juice
2 tbsp plain yogurt
1 tsp Indian chili powder
   or cayenne
1 tsp paprika
1 tsp ground coriander
1 tsp ground cumin
½ tsp salt
¼ tsp turmeric
1 tbsp tomato paste
1 tbsp olive oil

tikka
1½–2¼ lb (700 g–1 kg) firm white
   fish fillets, such as snapper or sea
   bass, cut into 1 in (3 cm) cubes

In a bowl, mix all the marinade ingredients together well. Add the fish pieces, gently mixing until they are well coated. Cover well and marinate in the refrigerator for at least 30 minutes, but preferably overnight.

Thread the fish onto the skewers, leaving a 2 in (5 cm) gap at each end for handling.

Cook on a hot grill or cast-iron griddle until opaque and golden on all sides, with slightly charred edges, 6–8 minutes. Serve with chutney.

Varra (lentil) kebabs

My mother would often make these for an Eastern version of afternoon tea, which we called chaa pani. Chaa pani is traditionally served to visiting guests and consists of a platter of various savories, accompanied by a selection of dipping sauces, apple chutney (page 162), and a cup of chaa (tea).

❤ Makes 18–20   ❤ Prep time: 20 mins   ❤ Cooking time: 20 mins

1 cup (200 g) mung dhal (dried split mung beans), soaked in water overnight
½ tsp green chili & cilantro paste (page 17)
1–2 garlic cloves, crushed
1 tomato, chopped
1 egg, beaten
¼ tsp freshly ground black pepper
¼ tsp turmeric
¼ tsp Indian chili powder or cayenne, or to taste
½ tsp ground cumin
½ tsp salt
4 tbsp gram (chickpea) flour
¼ tsp baking powder
vegetable oil, for frying

Rinse and drain the soaked dhal. Using a food processor or handheld immersion blender, blend the dhal to a thick paste. Transfer to a large bowl.

Add the green chili & cilantro paste, garlic, tomato, and the beaten egg, and mix well with a wooden spoon. Then add the black pepper, turmeric, chili powder, cumin, salt, gram flour, and baking powder to the mixture and mix well.

Pour the oil into a large pot to a depth of 2 in (5 cm). Heat until the surface shimmers and a small piece of bread turns golden. Working in batches, drop tablespoons of the mixture into the oil and fry for 6–8 minutes, turning from time to time, until golden on all sides.

Using a slotted spoon, transfer the kebabs to a plate lined with paper towels to drain excess oil. Serve hot.

Indian bread rolls

This dish isn't something I grew up with but is rather a more recent addition to my cooking. I developed this recipe with my mom and sister Anjum while trying to make savories to serve during Ramadan (the Muslim month of fasting). It makes a wonderful appetizer or finger food at a party.

❤ Makes 18–20   ❤ Prep time: 40 mins   ❤ Cooking time: 20 mins

filling
2 boneless chicken breasts
½ tbsp lemon juice
¼ cup (60 ml) olive oil
1 garlic clove, crushed
½ green bell pepper, finely diced
½ red bell pepper, finely diced
1 cup (140 g) frozen corn kernels,
   or a 14 oz (400 g) can corn kernels,
   drained
½ tsp ground cumin
½ tsp freshly ground black pepper
½ tsp green chili & cilantro paste
   (page 17)
3½ oz (100 g) cream cheese
½ cup (60 g) grated Cheddar cheese
salt

assembly
1 tbsp all-purpose flour
1–2 tsp warm water
1 loaf thinly sliced white bread,
   crusts removed
2 eggs, beaten
breadcrumbs, for coating
vegetable oil, for frying

tamarillo chutney (page 165),
   to serve

Place the chicken in a pot and add enough water to cover. Add ¼ teaspoon of salt and the lemon juice. Boil the chicken for approximately 30 minutes until the breasts are tender. Leave to cool for 10 minutes, then shred the flesh and set aside as you prepare the rest of the filling.

Wipe the pot clean, then add the oil, garlic, peppers, corn, cumin, black pepper, a pinch of salt, the green chili & cilantro paste, shredded chicken, and cream cheese. Cook over low heat for about 6 minutes to heat through, stirring with a wooden spoon. When the mixture is well combined, stir in the grated cheese and set aside to cool.

Assembly: In a small bowl, combine the flour and water to make a paste. Flatten the slices of bread lightly with a rolling pin. Put a slice of the rolled bread onto a board and place 2 heaped teaspoons of filling on one half of the slice. Spread the flour paste along the opposite three edges, fold over, and press down to seal. Repeat until all of the bread and filling has been used.

Place the beaten eggs and breadcrumbs in separate dishes. Dip each roll into the egg, then the breadcrumbs.

Pour the oil into a large pot to a depth of 2 in (5 cm). Heat until the surface shimmers and a small piece of bread turns golden. Working in batches, fry the rolls for 7–10 minutes, turning from time to time, until golden on all sides. Using a slotted spoon, transfer the cooked rolls to a plate lined with paper towels to drain excess oil.

Arrange on a platter and serve as an appetizer, with some tamarillo chutney alongside.

Ànjum's vegetable bhajias

This quick, easy vegetable fritter is my twin sister's recipe. Anjum first made it for us at a dinner party and we all loved it. The bhajias are perfect for a sharing platter, served with apple chutney (page 162). This dish has quickly become one of my favorite appetizers.

❤ Makes approx. 30   ❤ Prep time: 20 mins   ❤ Cooking time: 20 mins

2¼ lb (1 kg) frozen mixed vegetables (peas, carrots, and corn work best)
1 large potato, peeled and grated
1 small onion, finely diced
1 tsp salt
½ tsp turmeric
½ tsp ground cumin
½ tsp Indian chili powder or cayenne
1–2 garlic cloves, crushed
½ tsp ground coriander
½ tsp baking powder
4–6 tbsp gram (chickpea) flour
vegetable oil, for frying

Thaw the frozen vegetables under running water, drain well, and place in a large bowl. Use a potato masher or a handheld immersion blender to blend to a thick paste.

Using a wooden spoon or your hands, mix in the grated potato, then the onion, salt, turmeric, cumin, chili powder, garlic, coriander, baking powder, and 4 tbsp of the gram flour. Continue to mix until thoroughly combined and the mixture is the consistency of thick paste. Add the additional flour if the mixture is too runny.

Pour the oil into a large pot to a depth of 2 in (5 cm). Heat until the surface shimmers and a small piece of bread turns golden. Working in batches, drop tablespoons of the mixture into the oil and fry for 6–8 minutes, turning from time to time, until golden on all sides.

Using a slotted spoon, transfer the bhajias to a plate lined with paper towels to drain excess oil. Serve with chutney.

Curried chicken & pea pastries

These little pastries are a great way to cater for a large gathering; they are also great to have on hand for picnics, lunches, and unexpected guests. They can be made in advance and stored in the freezer; You can just pop them in the oven frozen and they are ready to serve in about 30 minutes. You can easily replace the chicken with cubed, parboiled potatoes for a vegetarian option.

❤ Makes 20–24   ❤ Prep time: 20 mins   ❤ Cooking time: 30 mins

1 tbsp olive oil
1 lb (500 g) ground chicken
1 tsp ground cumin
1 tsp ground coriander
¾ tsp turmeric
½–¾ tsp salt
pinch of freshly ground black
  pepper
½ cup (70 g) fresh or frozen peas
5–6 sheets ready-rolled puff pastry,
  partially defrosted
1 egg, beaten
handful toasted cumin seeds,
  for sprinkling

In a large sauté pan, heat the oil and brown the ground chicken. Add the spices, salt, and pepper, then stir in the peas. Stir for a minute or two, then cover and cook over low heat until the chicken is cooked. The mixture should be quite dry and clinging together. You may need to add a splash of water if the meat is sticking to the pan. Leave the mixture to cool before assembling the pastries.

Preheat the oven to 375°F (190°C) and line two large baking sheets with parchment paper.

Keep the pastry you're not using covered with a tea towel while you work. Cut the pastry sheets into 20–24 equal squares. Brush two adjacent corners of each square with beaten egg (since you will be bringing the corners together to make a triangle).

Spoon 3 heaped teaspoons of filling onto one half (on the diagonal) of each pastry square. Fold the pastry over to make a triangle, pressing the edges together with a fork. Brush the top with egg wash and sprinkle with the toasted cumin seeds, then arrange on the prepared baking pan.

Bake the pastries for 25–30 min or until puffed and golden. Serve with tomato chutney (page 162) or any chutney of your choice.

Light lunches

This section is full of easy dishes to pull together for a quick, inspired lunch or low-key meal for two. From my favorite masala omelet to spicy lamb kebabs in pita bread, these simple, flavorful recipes are perfect for when you're in a hurry but still want flavor and spice.

Masala omelet

This is perfect for a light, easy lunch or evenings you don't feel like cooking. You can make it as spicy as you like and use whatever you have in the refrigerator. This is the way I like to cook it.

❖ Serves 2   ❖ Prep time: 10 mins   ❖ Cooking time: 15 mins

½–1 tbsp vegetable oil
1 small onion, finely sliced
1–2 scallions, sliced
1 potato, peeled and cut into
   thin strips
½ bell pepper, diced
2–3 small mushrooms, sliced
4–5 eggs
¼ tsp ground cumin
¼ tsp ground coriander
½ tsp Indian chili powder
   or cayenne
salt and freshly ground black
   pepper
1 small tomato, diced
chopped cilantro, to serve (optional)

Heat the oil in an ovenproof frying pan. Sauté the onion until translucent, then add the scallions and continue to cook for a couple of minutes. Add the potatoes and fry over low–medium heat until they are golden and nearly cooked through, 4–5 minutes.

Add the peppers and then the mushrooms and cook, stirring occasionally, for a further 2–3 minutes.

In a bowl, whisk the eggs and then add all the spices. Season with salt and pepper.

Add the egg mixture to the frying pan, and let it cook until the bottom is set. Then add the diced tomato and place the frying pan under a hot broiler for 4–5 minutes or until golden and set.

Sprinkle with chopped herbs and serve on its own, or with roti (page 155) or paratha (page 157) and a tomato chutney (page 162).

Spicy scrambled eggs

This is one of my favorite ways to eat scrambled eggs and it always reminds me of my childhood in Malawi. We would come home for lunch after a morning at school and would be served this with hot roti (page 155).

Serves 4–6   Prep time: 15 mins   Cooking time: 15–20 mins

2–3 tbsp vegetable oil or ghee
4 onions, finely sliced
1–2 garlic cloves, crushed
8 eggs
½ tsp salt
½ tsp Indian chili powder
  or cayenne, plus extra for
  sprinkling
¼ tsp turmeric
¼ tsp ground cumin
½ tsp ground coriander
¼ tsp freshly ground black pepper,
  plus extra for sprinkling
1 green chili, finely sliced

In a large sauté pan, heat the oil or ghee and sauté the onions until soft and translucent. Add the garlic and cook for a further minute.

Meanwhile, beat the eggs in a large bowl and add all of the spices.

Add the green chili to the onions in the pan and continue to cook on low heat for about 5 minutes. Slowly add the beaten eggs, stirring continuously so they don't stick to the bottom of the pan.

When the eggs are scrambled and combined with the onions, cover, and continue cook over low heat for 8–10 minutes, stirring occasionally, until the eggs are fully cooked. Sprinkle with black pepper and red chili powder, if desired, and serve with hot roti.

Chili sweetcorn

This is an excellent quick meal and a perfect side dish. I often eat a bowlful as a snack if I'm craving tangy heat. In my opinion, this is the best way to eat corn.

Serves 2   **Prep time: 10 mins**   **Cooking time: 10 mins**

1–2 tbsp vegetable oil
1¾ cups (250 g) fresh, frozen or canned (drained) corn kernels
½ tsp salt
½ tsp Indian chili powder or cayenne
1 tbsp white vinegar
scant 1 cup (200 g) canned tomato purée or passata
lemon halves, for squeezing (grilled or fresh)
chopped cilantro, to garnish

In a sauté pan, heat the oil, then cook the corn, salt, and chili powder for about 5 minutes, stirring.

Add the vinegar and tomato purée or passata and simmer for about 10 minutes, or until the corn is tender.

Squeeze lemon juice over the chili corn and sprinkle with chopped cilantro before serving.

Potato curry

This is an easy, light lunch or supper, perfect for meat-free days. It was a staple for us growing up as a weekend breakfast or lunch, but for me it is perfect for any time of the day. Served with some hot roti (page 155), it makes a quick vegetarian meal.

❖ Serves 2—4   ❖ Prep time: 15 mins   ❖ Cooking time: 20—25 mins

¼ cup (60 ml) vegetable oil
4 large potatoes, peeled and diced
1 tsp salt
¼ tsp freshly ground black pepper
¼ tsp turmeric
¼ tsp ground cumin
¼ tsp garlic powder, or
   1 garlic clove, crushed
1 tsp Indian chili powder
   or cayenne (optional)

garnish
1 tsp vegetable oil
¼ tsp mustard seeds
¼ tsp crushed red pepper flakes

In a sauté pan, heat the oil over low heat, then cook the diced potatoes, salt, and spices until the potatoes are tender, 20—25 minutes. If they're catching on the bottom, add a small amount of water, but the aim is for a dry curry.

In a separate small pan, heat the oil and add the mustard seeds and red pepper flakes just until the seeds start popping. Remove from the heat and pour over the curry.

Serve with roti.

Curried okra & eggs

This is a great dish to cook if you are on your own or don't want a lot of fuss. Okra, also known as "lady's fingers," is a green flowering plant, rich in vitamins and fiber. This simple curry makes a perfect vegetarian dish, best served with roti (page 155), naan (page 153), or any toasted bread.

❖ Serves 2   ❖ Prep time: 10 mins   ❖ Cooking time: 15 mins

1 tbsp vegetable oil
2 tbsp tomato purée or passata
1 tbsp tomato paste
1 tsp Indian chili powder
  or cayenne
1 tsp ground coriander
½ tsp turmeric
½ tsp ground cumin
9 oz (250 g) okra (fresh or frozen),
  ends trimmed
3 hard-boiled eggs, peeled and
  halved lengthways
freshly ground black pepper

Heat the oil in a large sauté pan and add the tomato passata and paste. Then add the spices and cook, stirring over low heat until the oil looks like it is separating from the tomato mixture, about 5 minutes.

Add the okra to the tomato sauce and continue to cook for 5–6 minutes before adding the eggs. Cook over low heat for a further 5 minutes, until the okra is tender. Don't stir too much or you will break the eggs, but you can spoon the sauce over the eggs and okra to ensure they are evenly coated. Sprinkle with black pepper and serve.

Crunchy-topped potatoes & chickpeas with tamarind sauce

This is a lovely vegetarian dish that I grew up with; it was always served as a snack when we had visitors. I sometimes make it if I don't feel like having a big meal. It's spicy, crunchy, and tangy—a bowlful of goodness. Bombay or bhuja mix can be found in any Indian food store and many local supermarkets.

Serves 4   **Prep time: 20 mins**   **Cooking time: 30 mins**

1 tbsp vegetable oil
scant 1 cup (200 g) tomato purée
  or passata
½ tsp salt, plus extra for boiling
½–1 tsp Indian chili powder
  or cayenne
1 tsp paprika
1 tbsp tomato paste
1 tsp white vinegar
1 tbsp ketchup
approx. 1 lb (500 g) baby potatoes,
  peeled if you like, quartered
14 oz (400 g) can chickpeas, rinsed
  and drained
small bunch fresh cilantro, chopped
1 small red onion, chopped
handful Bombay or bhuja mix

sauce
3 tsp tamarind paste
4 tsp brown sugar
½ tsp ground cumin
5 tbsp water

For the tamarind sauce, combine all of the ingredients in a small saucepan and simmer until the sauce thickens, about 10 minutes. Allow to cool before serving. (This sauce tastes better the next day and keeps in the refrigerator for 1 month.)

In a large pot, heat the oil over medium heat, then add the tomato purée or passata, salt, chili powder, and paprika and cook for 2–3 minutes.

Add the tomato paste, vinegar, and ketchup and continue to cook on low heat for 10 minutes.

Meanwhile, parboil the potatoes in salted water for 8–10 minutes, then drain.

Remove a small handful of the potatoes and roughly mash them. Add these to the tomato mixture, along with the remaining potatoes and the chickpeas. Simmer for an additional 8–10 minutes until tender.

Spoon into small bowls and sprinkle with cilantro and red onion. Drizzle with tamarind sauce and serve with crunchy Bombay mix.

Spicy lamb kebabs in pita bread with crunchy salad & yogurt dip

I often serve these mid-week if I am pressed for time and we want something nutritious and healthy. You can prepare these in advance and freeze them, taking them out to thaw the night before. They are also great to serve at a summer gathering or barbecue, since people can help themselves and make their own sandwiches.

❧ Serves 4—6   ❧ Prep time: 20 mins   ❧ Cooking time: 30 mins

kebabs
2¼ lb (1 kg) ground lamb
2—3 garlic cloves, crushed
1 onion, peeled and finely chopped
1 heaped tsp ground cumin
1 heaped tsp ground coriander
1 heaped tsp turmeric
1—1½ tsp green chili & cilantro paste
    (page 17)
1 egg
½—¾ tsp salt
½ tsp freshly ground black pepper
breadcrumbs, if needed
2 tbsp olive oil

yogurt dip
¾—1 cup (200—300 g) plain
    Greek yogurt
2 tbsp chopped fresh mint
handful chopped fresh cilantro

to serve
4—6 small pitas, slit open on
    one side
lettuce leaves
sweet chili sauce, to serve

In a large bowl, combine the kebab ingredients, except for the breadcrumbs and oil, and mix well. The egg should bind it together, however, if the mixture is a little too wet, add a small amount of breadcrumbs. (To check the mixture is seasoned to your liking, fry a small amount and taste before you form the kebabs.)

Divide the meat mixture into approximately 20 evenly sized balls, then mold them into long sausage shapes. A great trick my mom taught me, which also makes the kebabs cook evenly, is to mold a ball around the handle of a wooden spoon so it is 3—4 in (8—10 cm) long (they will shrink when cooked), then gently slide it off the handle. You can make larger or smaller kebabs if you like, just adjust the cooking time accordingly.

When you are ready to cook, lightly coat a frying pan or griddle pan with some of the olive oil and place over low—medium heat. Working in batches, fry the kebabs for 8—10 minutes, turning occasionally, until cooked through. You can also cook them on a baking sheet in an oven preheated to 425°F (220°C) for 10—12 min, or grill them for 15—20 minutes.

For the pita bread, preheat the oven to 400°F (200°C). Stack the pitas and wrap them tightly in foil. Heat for 5—8 min, then set aside, still covered in foil, to keep warm.

For the dip, place the yogurt in a bowl and add the mint and cilantro. Stir to combine.

Fill each pita with some the lettuce and a few kebabs, then spoon yogurt and sweet chili sauce over the top.

Spicy corn on the cob

A perfect summer side dish, but beware of messy fingers, and that one is never enough.

❧ Serves 3–4 ❧ Prep time: 10 mins ❧ Cooking time: 10 mins

3 ears of corn
2 tbsp vegetable oil
½ tsp Indian chili powder
  or cayenne
½ tsp salt
½ tsp crushed red pepper flakes
1 tsp white vinegar

Husk the corn, cut each cob in half, and boil in salted water until tender, about 5 minutes. Or you can microwave the corn, in their husks, for about 3 minutes on each side before husking and halving them.

In a large, deep frying pan, heat the oil, chili powder, salt, red pepper flakes, and vinegar. Sizzle for about a minute, taking care not to burn the spices, then add the cooked corn cobs.

Turn to evenly coat the cobs, and leave on the heat for a couple of minutes. Serve hot.

Roasted vegetable & haloumi salad with cilantro & chili dressing

I created this salad to celebrate some amazing seasonal vegetables and their vibrant colors. Salty fried haloumi is delicious with the sweetness of the roasted veggies, and the dressing gives it all a great kick.

❧ Serves 4–6   ❧ Prep time: 20 mins   ❧ Cooking time: 30 mins

2 parsnips
2 beets
2 sweet potatoes
3 carrots
7 oz (200 g) haloumi or paneer
1 head Bibb, butter, or romaine
  lettuce, leaves torn
olive oil, for drizzling
salt and freshly ground
  black pepper

dressing
4–5 tbsp olive oil
1 tsp balsamic vinegar
juice of ½ a lemon
3 tbsp chopped fresh cilantro
2 tsp liquid honey
1–2 garlic cloves, crushed
1 tsp crushed red pepper flakes

Preheat the oven to 350°F (180°C).

Peel and chop parsnips, beets, sweet potatoes, and carrots into ¾ in (2 cm) chunks. Place them in a large baking dish or roasting pan and drizzle with enough olive oil to lightly coat. Roast for about 45 minutes until cooked and golden.

Meanwhile, thinly slice the haloumi or paneer and pat dry with paper towels. Heat a dry nonstick frying pan over medium heat and, working in batches if necessary, fry the haloumi slices until golden on both sides. Set aside to cool.

Place all of the dressing ingredients together in a blender, blend well, and season with salt and pepper. You can add a little more salt, lemon juice, or chili according to your taste.

When the vegetables are cooked, let them cool to room temperature before assembling your salad. Place the lettuce leaves in a large dish, along with the roast vegetables, and mix gently.

Scatter the haloumi or paneer on top, and drizzle with the dressing.

Farha's Middle Eastern-style salad

This is a gorgeous salad, inspired by the flavors of the Middle East. My sister Farha lives in Abu Dhabi, and I first had this salad on one of my trips to visit her. She put it together easily and served it with some succulent roasted lamb. It goes beautifully with any Eastern-flavored meat dish but is just as good on its own as a light meal. It is my go-to when I am asked to bring a dish to share at a dinner party. It's light, fresh, and beautifully flavored.

❖ Serves 4–6   ❖ Prep time: 20 mins   ❖ Cooking time: 20 mins

1 eggplant, cut into ½ in
   (1 cm) cubes
4 tbsp olive oil, plus exra for frying
3 flatbreads, such as pita, cut into
   small squares
3 bell peppers (red, yellow, and
   green), deseeded and cut into
   ½ in (1 cm) cubes
2 large tomatoes, diced
3–4 scallions, sliced
small bunch flat-leaf parsley,
   chopped
¼ cup (25 g) mint leaves, chopped
seeds of half a pomegranate
salt and freshly ground black
   pepper

pomegranate dressing
3 tbsp pomegranate molasses
3 tbsp olive oil
juice of ½ a lemon
2 tsp brown sugar

Preheat the oven to 350°F (180°C).

Spread the eggplant on a baking tray, drizzle with the olive oil, and bake until cooked and golden, 12–15 minutes.

Lightly coat the base of a frying pan with oil and fry the bread pieces until golden and crispy. Transfer to a plate lined with a paper towels to drain excess oil and season with salt and pepper.

In a large salad bowl, combine the eggplant, peppers, tomatoes, scallions, parsley, and mint. Toss together.

Place all of the dressing ingredients in a jar and shake to combine. Add the dressing to the salad and mix again. Add the fried flatbread just before serving, so it stays crisp. Garnish with pomegranate seeds.

Masala baked beans

A perfect meal for one, and a great way to add a little spice to your baked beans. Once you have tried this recipe you won't want to eat baked beans any other way.

❖❖ Serves 1–2   ❖❖ Prep time: 10 mins   ❖❖ Cooking time: 10 mins

olive oil, for frying
1 onion, diced
½ garlic clove, crushed
14 oz (400 g) can baked beans
½ tsp Indian chili powder
   or cayenne
½ tsp ground coriander
¼ tsp ground cumin
1–2 eggs, fried or poached
   (optional)
salt and freshly ground black
   pepper

Heat a little oil in a frying pan and sauté the onion and garlic until soft but not browned, then add the baked beans. Stir, then mix in the spices. Cook over low heat until the the beans are heated through. Taste and season with salt and pepper.

Place the eggs on top, if using, and serve with toasted bread, roti (page 155) or paratha (page 157).

Spicy peppers in tomato sauce

There is nothing boring about this pepper dish. It is crunchy, sweet, and full of flavor. Mom always served this with vegetable pulau (page 138), but it also goes beautifully with meat dishes and makes a tasty light lunch with flatbread.

❖ Serves 4–6   ❖ Prep time: 10 mins   ❖ Cooking time: 15 mins

1 tbsp olive oil
¼ tsp cumin seeds
¼ tsp mustard seeds
3 bell peppers, deseeded and sliced
4 tbsp tomato purée or passata
¼ tsp turmeric
¼ tsp ground coriander
¼ tsp garlic powder
¼ tsp ground cumin
¼ tsp salt

Heat the oil in a sauté pan and add the cumin and mustard seeds. When they start changing color, add the peppers and cook for 5 minutes.

Add the tomato purée or passata, all of the spices, and the salt.

Cook, stirring occasionally, over low–medium heat for 10 minutes or until the peppers are cooked.

Burtho

I love this curried dip, although I must admit, as a child when my mom used to make it—or even suggest it was on the menu for dinner—my sister and I would wrinkle our noses and whine! As children, texture and appearance are an important part of what we like, and back then I didn't like the texture of eggplants. Now, as an adult, this is one of my favorite dishes.

∙∙∙ Serves 4–6   **∙∙∙ Prep time: 15 mins**   **∙∙∙ Cooking time: 30 mins**

1 large eggplant
2–3 tbsp olive oil
1 onion, sliced
scant 1 cup (200 g) tomato purée
  or passata
2–3 garlic cloves, crushed
¼ tsp salt
¼ tsp turmeric
¼ tsp ground cumin
¼ tsp paprika
½ tsp Indian chili powder
  or cayenne

to serve
crushed pistachios or other nuts
whole cumin seeds
sourdough bread, toasted or grilled
  if you like

Using a fork, poke holes all over the eggplant and put it in an oven dish under a hot broiler. Broil, turning it regularly, for about 15 minutes, until it is soft. You will be able to tell it is ready since it will split open; the flesh needs to be mushy. Set aside until just cool enough to handle.

Meanwhile, heat the oil in a large sauté pan, and fry the onion until pale golden.

Add the tomato purée or passata, garlic, salt, and all of the spices, and simmer on low heat for 10–15 minutes.

Holding the eggplant by the stalk, remove the skin with a spoon, and roughly mash the flesh with a fork. Discard the stalk and skin.

Mix the eggplant flesh into the tomato mixture and continue to cook over low heat for a further 5–7 minutes.

Sprinkle with crushed nuts and whole cumin seeds and serve with sourdough bread.

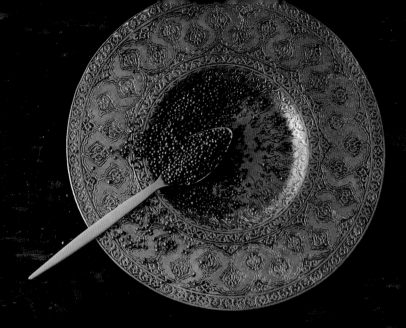

The main event

I have created these dishes to cater for any occasion—from an everyday meal to a festive family gathering. Whether you want a simple curry or an elaborate dinner, you will find inspiration in all of these recipes.

Chili-crusted baked salmon

This is a great recipe to serve at a large gathering. You can prepare it beforehand and have it ready to go in the oven. It is perfect with Anjum's spicy roast potatoes (page 151) or a crisp green salad.

🌿 Serves 6–8   🌿 Prep time: 20 mins   🌿 Cooking time: 30–40 mins

**1 skin-on side of salmon
  (approx. 2¼ lb/1 kg)**
1 tbsp olive oil
½–1 tsp crushed red pepper flakes
**salt and freshly ground black
  pepper**
good squeeze lemon juice

to serve
lemon or lime wedges
salad greens
**microgreens or edible flowers
  (optional)**

Preheat the oven to 400°F (200°C).

Remove any bones from your salmon. Rinse the fish under cold running water and pat-dry with paper towels.

Cut a piece of foil about twice the size of a large baking pan. Lay half of it on the pan, making sure there is enough foil to completely cover the salmon. Place salmon on the foil, skin side down.

In a jar, combine the oil, red pepper flakes, salt, pepper, and lemon juice and shake well to combine. Taste for seasoning. You may want to add a touch more red pepper flakes flakes or lemon juice. Drizzle over the salmon.

Cover the salmon with the foil, making sure the edges of the foil are rolled together to seal the fish in a parcel.

Bake for 30–40 minutes or until the salmon is just cooked through but still moist.

Serve on a bed of salad greens, sprinkled with microgreens or edible flowers, with lemon or lime wedges for squeezing.

Mom's chicken biryani

This is a family favorite, usually made for special occasions, since it has a lot of ingredients and is quite time-consuming, but it is surprisingly easy to make and tastes divine. The key to a good biryani is an intensely flavored meat, seafood, or vegetable with not too much gravy, and perfect fluffy rice. I have chosen to use chicken since it is easy to work with. Serve it with cucumber raita (page 167).

❊ Serves 8–10   ❊ Prep time: 30–40 mins   ❊ Cooking time: 1–1½ hours

vegetable oil, for frying
5–6 potatoes, peeled and halved
2 onions, sliced
2 in (5 cm) piece cinnamon stick
2–3 whole cardamom pods
2–3 whole cloves
4–6 whole black peppercorns
1 tsp cumin seeds
3 tsp ground coriander
½ tsp turmeric
1 tsp ground cumin
1–2 tsp Indian chili powder
  or cayenne
2 tsp paprika
2¼ cups (525 g) tomato purée
2–3 garlic cloves, crushed
4½ lb (2 kg) boneless, skinless
  chicken thighs, diced
1 tbsp tomato paste
1 tbsp white vinegar
4 cups (800 g) basmati rice, soaked
  in water for 20 minutes
1 tbsp olive oil
1 tbsp butter or ghee, plus extra for
  sprinkling
8 cups (2 liters) boiling water
4 hard-boiled eggs, peeled and
  halved lengthways
¼ tsp saffron
red and yellow food coloring
handful of chopped cilantro
salt and ground black pepper

Heat ¾ cup (180 ml) of vegetable oil in a frying pan and fry the potatoes until golden. Drain on a plate lined with paper towels.

In a large saucepan heat ½ cup (120 ml) of vegetable oil and fry the onions until golden. Transfer to a plate lined with paper towels to drain. Add the whole spices to the same oil and fry for 1 minute, then add ground spices, tomato purée, garlic, and 1½ teaspoons of salt, and cook over low heat for 6–8 minutes.

Add the chicken to the spices and continue to cook, covered, for a further 10 minutes. Add the tomato paste, vinegar, and fried potatoes and simmer until the sauce clings to the meat, 15–20 minutes. If the chicken catches on the bottom, add a splash of water. Once the chicken is cooked, turn the heat off.

Rinse and drain the soaked rice. In a large pot, heat the olive oil and butter or ghee, add the rice, and stir until it just starts to become translucent, then add the boiling water and 4 teaspoons of salt. Allow to boil for 1–2 minutes, turn the heat down to low, and cook, covered, for 12–14 minutes until tender.

Place half of the curry into a large karahi (Indian wok) or pot. Mix about 1 cup of the cooked rice with a few drops of food coloring and set aside. Layer half of the white rice on top of the curry in the pot, then a layer of the remaining curry, and top with the remaining white rice. Scatter the top layer with the colored rice, fried onions, and boiled eggs. Mix the saffron with a splash of water and sprinkle on top, along with the cilantro.

Mix a little more oil and ghee and drizzle this around the edges so it drips down the sides of the biryani, cover the pot, and cook over low heat for 15–20 min. Serve hot.

Chili-basted roast chicken

Roast chicken is one of our favorite family meals—we usually make it on a Sunday, with all the trimmings. This fusion-style recipe offers a different take on traditional roast chicken. Serve it with cassava fries (page 149) for an interesting change from the usual roasted vegetable accompaniment.

Serves 4–6   Prep time: 20 mins   Cooking time: 90 mins

juice of ½ a lemon
1 tsp salt
4–5 garlic cloves, crushed
3 lb (1.4 kg) whole chicken,
    preferably organic
1 tsp freshly ground black pepper
2 tsp paprika
1 tsp Indian chili powder
    or cayenne
1 tsp ground cumin
½ tsp ground coriander
3 tbsp olive oil
2 tsp tomato paste

to garnish
red and green chilies, thinly sliced
fresh cilantro sprigs
lime wedges

Combine lemon juice with half of the salt and half of the garlic. Smear over the chicken and set aside to marinate for 20 minutes.

Meanwhile, prepare chili mixture. In a small bowl, combine the remaining garlic and salt with the pepper, paprika, chili powder, cumin, coriander, and oil. Mix well then add the tomato paste.

Place a roasting pan or dish in the oven and preheat to 400°F (200°C).

Drain the chicken of the lemon marinade and smear with the chili mixture, making sure it is well coated. Place the chicken in the hot roasting dish, cover with foil, and roast for 30 minutes. Remove the foil, baste the chicken with the pan juices, and return to the oven. Continue to roast until the chicken is crisp but moist and the juices run clear, 30–40 minutes.

If you are making cassava fries, do this about 10 minutes before the chicken is done.

Transfer the chicken to a serving dish and garnish with sliced chilies, cilantro sprigs, and lime wedges. Make sure the chicken has rested for 10–15 minutes before carving.

Nini's nutty chicken

This is my sister Nishat's recipe (we call her Nini), and every time I make this I think of her. This dish is creamy and nutty and gorgeous—perfect for a special dinner. Serve with saffron rice (page 143) and naan (page 153).

❧ Serves 4–6   ❧ Prep time: 20 mins   ❧ Cooking time: 30 mins

2 tbsp vegetable oil
3 large onions, sliced
1–2 tsp green chili & cilantro paste (page 17)
2–3 garlic cloves, crushed
¼ tsp ground cumin
8 bone-in chicken pieces, skin removed
scant 1 cup (200 g) canned diced tomatoes
¼ tsp turmeric
½ tsp salt
3 tbsp crushed mixed nuts (pistachios, almonds, cashews)
scant ½ cup (100 ml) heavy cream

In a large pot, heat the oil and sauté the onions until soft and translucent. Add the green chili & cilantro paste, garlic, and cumin, and then the chicken pieces. Cook for 15 minutes on low heat.

Add the tomatoes, turmeric, salt, and 2 tablespoons of the crushed nuts, and cook for another 15–20 minutes or until the chicken is cooked.

Just before serving, stir in the cream. Garnish with the remaining mixed nuts.

Butter chicken

This is my version of everyone's favorite Indian curry. My recipe is a simplified version of Murgh Makhanim, a buttery Moghul dish that is full of flavor but nothing like the butter chicken you might find in Indian restaurants. Serve it with rice and homemade roti (page 155).

❧ Serves 4–6   ❧ Prep time: 15 mins   ❧ Cooking time: 30–40 mins

marinade
1 cup (140 g) plain yogurt
1 tsp salt
1 tsp garam masala
1 tsp Indian chili powder or cayenne
½ tbsp vegetable oil
3–4 garlic cloves, crushed
small piece of fresh ginger, grated
juice of ½ a lemon
pinch of saffron (optional)
1 lb 12 oz (800 g) boneless chicken
  breasts, cubed

curry
5 tbsp (75 g) butter
2–3 whole cardamom pods
piece of cinnamon stick
2–3 whole cloves
2–3 garlic cloves, crushed
small piece fresh ginger, grated
1–2 green chilies, chopped
  (optional)
4 large tomatoes, puréed,
  or a 14 oz (400 g) can tomato
  purée or passata
1 tbsp tomato paste
1 tsp salt
1 tsp garam masala
2 tbsp honey
½–¾ cup (120–180 ml) heavy
  cream
handful chopped fresh cilantro

In a large bowl, mix all of the marinade ingredients together and rub onto the chicken pieces. Cover and refrigerate for at least 1 hour but preferably overnight.

When ready to cook, preheat the oven to 400°F (200°C). Spread the marinated chicken out on a baking pan and roast for 25–30 minutes until cooked through.

To make the curry, melt the butter in a large pot and add the whole spices, garlic, ginger, and green chilies and stir. Add the tomatoes and tomato paste, cover, and cook over low heat for 10–15 minutes.

Stir in the salt, garam masala, and honey. Add the chicken and any pan juices to the pot. Cover and simmer for 10 minutes.

Lastly, add the cream and chopped cilantro and remove from the heat. Serve with plain rice and roti.

Coconut chicken curry

This easy, delicious curry is one of my mother's signature dishes we grew up with. Eating it always brings back childhood memories. It's fresh, with a slight kick, and perfect to serve at a gathering.

 Serves 4   Prep time: 15 mins   Cooking time: 30–40 mins

1 tbsp vegetable oil
3 onions, sliced
1 lb (500 g) boneless chicken
   breasts, cubed
1–2 tsp green chili & cilantro paste
   (page 17)
2–3 garlic cloves, crushed
1 tsp salt
scant 1 cup (200 g) canned diced
   tomatoes
1 tsp ground coriander
½ tsp ground cumin
½ tsp ground turmeric
1 cup (240 ml) coconut milk

to garnish
chopped cilantro
grated coconut (fresh or dried)

Heat the oil in a medium saucepan or lidded frying pan over medium heat and sauté the onions until softened and translucent.

Add the chicken, chili & cilantro paste, garlic, and salt and cook, stirring occasionally, for 5–10 minutes.

Add the tomatoes and spices, cover, and simmer for a further 15–20 minutes until the chicken is cooked.

Add the coconut milk and simmer over low heat until heated through. Serve, garnished with cilantro and coconut, accompanied by basmati rice and naan bread (page 153) or poppadums.

Spicy chili shrimp

Easily the best chili shrimp this side of the Pacific! These are perfect to serve for a special occasion. For extra impact, Mom sometimes used shell-on jumbo shrimp. Serve with fried potatoes.

Serves 4–6   Prep time: 15 mins   Cooking time: 15–20 mins

2¼ lb (1 kg) raw peeled shrimp, deveined
5 tbsp (75 g) butter
dash of vegetable oil
3–4 garlic cloves, thinly sliced
½ tsp crushed red pepper flakes
2 tbsp ketchup
handful chopped fresh cilantro

marinade
juice of 1 lemon
1 tsp salt
freshly ground black pepper
1 tbsp vegetable oil
1 tsp Indian chili powder or cayenne
1 tsp paprika

In a bowl, combine the marinade ingredients. Rinse the shrimp, and drain them very well before adding to the marinade, turning to coat them well. Refrigerate for 30–60 minutes to marinate.

When you are ready to cook, drain the excess marinade from the shrimp.

In a large frying pan, heat the butter with a dash of oil over medium heat. Add the sliced garlic and cook until pale golden, then add the red pepper flakes and shrimp. Turn the heat down to low and cook for 6–8 minutes.

Add the ketchup and cook for a further 2–3 minutes, just until the shrimp are cooked—they will be pink and opaque. Make sure you don't overcook them or they will get rubbery and hard to chew.

Sprinkle with chopped cilantro before serving.

Slow-cooked mild lamb curry

This is a superb, easy curry that will appeal to those in the family who prefer milder heat (like my children). I have given methods to cook this on the stovetop, in the oven, or using a slow cooker. It's beautifully spiced, but you can add more crushed red pepper flakes if you want it spicier. Serve it with basmati rice and roti (page 155), and cucumber raita (page 167).

❈ Serves 4–6   ❈ Prep time: 15 mins   ❈ Cooking time: 1 hr 10 mins

2–3 tbsp vegetable oil
2–3 medium onions, finely sliced
1½ lb (700 g) boneless lamb
  shoulder, fat removed, cubed
1½ tsp ground cumin
1½ tsp ground coriander
1 tsp turmeric
½–1 tsp crushed red pepper flakes
  (optional)
3–4 garlic cloves, finely chopped
1 tsp finely chopped fresh ginger
⅔–scant 1 cup (150–200 ml)
  chicken or beef stock
scant 1 cup (200 ml) heavy cream
1 tsp salt, or to taste
½ tsp freshly ground black pepper
fresh cilantro, to garnish (optional)

Heat the oil over medium heat in a Dutch oven or heavy-based pan with a lid (oven-safe if you plan to cook in the oven). Add the onions and cook until pale and just starting to color. Add the lamb and brown on all sides.

Add the spices, red pepper flakes (if using), garlic, and ginger, and cook for a couple of minutes until well combined.

Add the stock and cream and season with the salt and pepper. Bring to a boil then turn the heat down, cover, and simmer for 1 hour, or until the meat is tender. Alternatively, preheat the oven to 300°F (150°C) and cook for 1 hour until the meat is tender, or cook in a slow cooker on low for 5–6 hours.

Garnish with cilantro and serve with rice, roti, and a refreshing cucumber raita on the side, if desired.

Ketchup chicken

This dish brings back so many memories of my childhood in Malawi. This was a regular meal during the week since it is so simple to make. It's best eaten with a crusty loaf of fresh bread, although you can serve it with rice, too. It's sweet and tangy, with a hint of chili.

❧ Serves 4–6   ❧ Prep time: 10 mins   ❧ Cooking time: 30 mins

8 large chicken drumsticks
1 tsp garlic powder
1 tsp Indian chili powder
or cayenne (optional)
½ tsp salt
1¾ cups (420 g) ketchup
2–3 tbsp vegetable oil
4 onions, sliced

Place the chicken in a large bowl, add the garlic, chili powder, salt, and ketchup, and marinate in the refrigerator for 30 minutes.

When you are ready to cook, heat the oil in a large pot or sauté pan over low–medium heat. Add the onions and cook for about 10 minutes, just until they are translucent and lightly golden (it is very important not to overcook them; you have to watch this process carefully).

Add the marinated chicken, turn down the heat to low, and cook, covered, for about 20 minutes, until the chicken is cooked through.

Serve with crusty bread or basmati rice.

Roast lamb with a chili rub

This is one of my favorite ways to make roast leg of lamb and a lovely Indian twist on the traditional Western roast dinner. It is perfect for a family gathering. You can serve this with Anjum's spicy roast potatoes (page 151), seasonal vegetables, and cilantro chutney (page 162) to make the perfect celebration meal.

 Serves 6   Prep time: 20 mins   Cooking time: 4 hours

3 lb 5 oz–4½ lb (1.5–2 kg) leg
  of lamb
1 tsp salt
2–3 garlic cloves, crushed
1 tsp grated fresh ginger
juice of 1 lemon
4–5 tbsp olive oil
1 tsp ground cumin
1 tsp Indian chili powder
  or cayenne
2 tsp paprika
1 tsp ground coriander
cilantro sprigs, to garnish

Prick the lamb all over with a fork and use a small knife to make small cuts all over. In a bowl, mix the salt, garlic, ginger, lemon juice, oil, and spices and rub it all over the lamb. Cover well and leave to marinate in the refrigerator overnight.

The next day, bring the lamb to room temperature. Preheat the oven to 350°F (180°C).

Place the lamb in a large roasting pan and cover completely with foil, making sure there is no room for any steam to come out.

Roast in the oven for 3½–4 hours, until the lamb is tender and falling off the bone. If you like, you can uncover the lamb for the final 30 minutes to brown the top.

Garnish with cilantro sprigs and serve with Anjum's spicy roast potatoes, cilantro chutney, and seasonal vegetables.

Machi fry

Growing up, this was a staple on the menu. Mom and Dad loved it (us girls weren't so sure) but as an adult, it's one of those dishes that I have really enjoyed making and serving. It's so easy to whip up and a great crowd-pleaser. Serve it with rice or hot roti (page 155) or paratha (page 157).

✿ Serves 4–6   ✿ Prep time: 15 mins   ✿ Cooking time: 25 min

1¾–2¼ lb (800 g–1 kg) firm white
   fish fillets, such as cod, haddock,
   or snapper, skin removed
2–3 tbsp vegetable oil
2 onions, sliced
1¼ cups (300 g) tomato purée
   or passata
2 tsp ground coriander
1 tsp paprika
1 tsp Indian chili powder
   or cayenne
½ tsp ground cumin
½ tsp turmeric
1 garlic clove, crushed
½ tsp salt
grind of black pepper
chopped cilantro, to garnish

Cut the fish fillets into 8–12 large pieces.

In a large karahi (Indian wok) or frying pan heat the oil over medium heat. Add the onions and cook until golden (being careful not to burn them). Using a slotted spoon, transfer to a plate lined with paper towels to drain excess oil.

In the same oil, fry the fish pieces in batches, until golden, 6–8 minutes. Then transfer to another plate lined with paper towels.

Add the tomato purée or passata to the pan, along with the spices, salt, and pepper, and cook until the oil and tomato appear to separate, about 15 minutes.

Gently place the fish back in the pan, giving the pan a gentle shake, making sure you don't break the fish. Cook for a further 5–10 minutes, to ensure the fish is coated in the sauce.

Transfer to a serving dish and scatter with the fried onions and fresh cilantro. Serve with rice or hot roti or paratha.

Pea & paneer curry

A perfect vegetarian dish that is sweet and creamy. Paneer is a mild Indian fresh cheese made by curdling hot milk with lemon juice. Because it is quite bland, it works really well with rich, spicy sauces. You can make this with mushrooms or cauliflower as well. Serve with turmeric rice (page 144).

Serves 4–6   Prep time: 15 mins   Cooking time: 30–40 mins

1 block paneer (approx. 14 oz/400 g)
2–3 tbsp vegetable oil
1 red onion, sliced
1 yellow onion, finely chopped
1–2 garlic cloves, crushed
½ tsp salt
3 tomatoes, diced
½ tsp turmeric
½ tsp ground cumin
1½ tsp ground coriander
½ tsp paprika
1½ tsp Indian chili powder
  or cayenne
¾ cup tomato purée or passata
1 lb (500 g) baby peas
  (frozen is fine)
¼ cup (60 ml) heavy cream
cilantro sprigs, to garnish

Cut the paneer into 3–4 strips. Heat a dry nonstick sauté pan over medium heat and fry the paneer until golden on all sides. Chop into approximately 1 in (3 cm) cubes and set aside.

In the same pan, heat the oil over medium heat and fry the red onion slices until browned. Transfer to a plate lined with paper towels, leaving 1–2 tablespoons of oil in the pan (add a little oil if needed).

In the same pan, sauté the yellow onion over medium heat until translucent. Add the garlic, salt, and diced tomatoes, and cook, stirring occasionally, for 6–8 minutes.

Add the spices and the tomato purée or passata, and cook, covered, for a further 10 minutes, until the oil separates.

Add the peas and continue to simmer until they are tender. Lastly add the fried paneer and the cream. Simmer for 5–6 minutes until heated through. Garnish with the fried onions and cilantro sprigs, and serve hot, with turmeric rice.

Baked masala fish

This is a great dish to serve at a gathering. It doesn't take a lot of preparation, but it tastes divine and will impress your family and friends. It can be cooked on a grill, too, so it is perfect for easy summer entertaining. Serve with homemade fries.

❀ Serves 4–6   ❀ Prep time: 30 mins   ❀ Cooking time: 25–30 mins

4–6 lb (1.8–2.7 kg) whole fish, such as sea bass or snapper, gutted and scaled
crushed red pepper flakes, to serve
lemon wedges, to serve

marinade
1 tsp Indian chili powder or cayenne
1 tsp paprika
1 tsp ground coriander
1 tsp ground cumin
½ tsp freshly ground black pepper
½ tsp salt
1–2 garlic cloves, crushed
⅔ cup (150 ml) olive oil
a good squeeze of lemon juice
1 tbsp tomato purée or passata

Mix the marinade ingredients together and spread over the fish. Marinate in the refrigerator for 30 minutes.

Preheat the oven to 350°F (180°C) or heat your grill.

To bake, place the fish on a baking pan, cover with a large piece of foil, and bake for 20–25 minutes or until the fish is opaque. Remove the foil and bake for a further 5–10 minutes to crisp and brown the skin.

To grill, wrap the fish in foil and grill for 10–12 minutes on each side, until the fish is opaque, then remove the foil and brown for an additional 2 minutes on each side

Sprinkle with red pepper flakes if desired, and serve with lemon wedges. Perfect!

Chundo with currie & kitchrie

Chundo (ground lamb curry) is one of my favorite winter comfort foods. My sister Anjum makes it the best, and whenever she makes it for her family, she keeps a bowl for me in the refrigerator. This recipe consists of three separate components: chundo, currie (a yogurt sauce), and kitchrie (rice cooked with split black gram). They are best eaten in combination. Absolutely delicious!

꧁ Serves 4–6   ꧁ Prep time: 30 mins   ꧁ Cooking time: 1 hour

1 portion kitchrie (page 141)

chundo (ground lamb curry)
1 tbsp vegetable oil
1 small onion, finely sliced
2–3 garlic cloves, crushed
1 tsp salt
1 lb (500 g) ground chicken or lamb
14 oz (400 g) can diced tomatoes
1 tbsp tomato paste
1 tsp Indian chili powder or cayenne
1 tsp ground coriander
¼ tsp ground cumin
¼ tsp turmeric
¼ tsp garam masala
¼ cup (35 g) fresh or frozen peas
½ cup (50 g) sliced green beans

currie (yogurt sauce)
2 cups (500 g) plain yogurt
1⅔ cups (400 ml) cold water
1 tbsp gram (chickpea) flour
1 tbsp vegetable oil
¼ tsp salt
½ tsp Indian chili powder or cayenne
½ tsp ground coriander
½ tsp turmeric
1–2 tsp green chili & cilantro paste
   (page 17)
1 tsp tomato paste
fresh cilantro or curry leaves
   (optional), to garnish

Prepare the kitchrie and set aside.

For the chundo, heat the oil in a lidded pot over medium heat. Sauté the onion until translucent, then add the garlic, salt, and ground meat. Cook until the meat has browned, then add the tomatoes, tomato paste, and the spices. Turn down the heat and simmer for 15 minutes. Add the peas and beans and continue to simmer fo 5 more minutes, or until the meat and vegetables are cooked and the chundo is the consistency of thick soup; if you find you need more sauce, add a little water and simmer for 10 minutes more. Set aside.

Next, make the currie: In a bowl combine the yogurt, water, and flour and whisk until it all blends together. Set aside.

Heat the oil in a large pot over low–medium heat. Add the salt, spices, and cilantro & chili paste. Cook gently for 30 seconds, making sure the oil is not too hot or the spices will burn. Add a tablespoon of water, cook for another minute and then add the tomato paste, stirring well. Add the yogurt mixture.

Turn up the heat and bring the yogurt to a simmer—the color will change to a golden yellow. Simmer for 3–4 minutes, give it a quick stir with a whisk, and then turn off the heat.

To serve, spoon the kitchrie into individual pasta bowls, then add a spoonful of chundo. Make a well and add a ladleful (or more) of the currie, garnish with cilantro or curry leaves, and serve hot.

Crispy fried chicken

Who doesn't like fried chicken? This is lovely and crunchy with a touch of spice. And the great thing is you can bake it, for a lighter option.

❉ Serves 4–6 ❉ Prep time: 20 mins ❉ Cooking time: 20 mins

2–3 garlic cloves, crushed
1 small piece ginger, finely chopped
½ tsp salt
1 tsp white vinegar
6 chicken legs (thigh and drumstick)
vegetable or canola oil, for frying

coating
½ cup (60 g) dried breadcrumbs
4 tbsp all-purpose flour
2 tbsp cornstarch
¼ tsp salt
¼ tsp freshly ground black pepper
½ tsp Indian chili powder or cayenne
½ tsp paprika
½–¾ cup (120–180 ml) buttermilk

In a large pot, combine the garlic, ginger, salt, vinegar, chicken, and enough water to cover. Bring to a boil and then simmer for 20 minutes. Drain and set the chicken aside to cool slightly.

In a large ziplock bag, combine all of the coating ingredients except for the buttermilk, and mix well.

Put the buttermilk in a shallow bowl.

Dip one chicken leg in the buttermilk and then place it in the bag. Dip another and repeat, but don't have more than two chicken pieces in the bag at one time. Coat well and place on a baking tray or dish. Repeat until all of the chicken is well coated.

Pour the oil into a large pot or karahi (Indian wok) to a depth of 2 in (5 cm); it should be no more than two-thirds full. Heat until the surface shimmers and a small piece of bread turns golden. Working in batches, fry the chicken pieces for 6–8 minutes, turning from time to time, until golden on all sides. Transfer to a plate lined with paper towels to drain excess oil.

Alternatively, to oven-fry: Preheat the oven to 350°F (180°C). Place the chicken on a baking tray and drizzle with olive oil. Bake for 20–30 minutes, until golden, turning them once halfway through the cooking time.

Serve with spicy potato wedges or spicy roasted potatoes (page 151).

Simple chicken curry

This is one of those beautiful Indian curries that is simple, easy, and a staple in any Indian kitchen. Every Indian family has their own method and their own blend of spices they like to use—this is ours.

❀ Serves 4   ❀ Prep time: 20 mins   ❀ Cooking time: 1 hour

2 tbsp vegetable oil
1 onion, sliced
1 lb 5 oz (600 g) bone-in chicken
   pieces
2–3 garlic cloves, crushed
¾ tsp salt
2 potatoes, peeled and quartered
1½ tsp ground coriander
1 tsp ground cumin
¼ tsp turmeric
1 tsp Indian chili powder
   or cayenne
½ tsp paprika (optional)
4 tbsp tomato purée or passata
1 tbsp tomato paste
1½ cups (350 ml) boiling water
chopped fresh cilantro,
   to garnish

In a large pot, heat the oil over medium heat and sauté the onion until translucent, then add the chicken pieces, garlic, and salt and cook, turning the chicken occasionally, for 10 minutes.

Add the potatoes and cook for a further 10 minutes. Add all of the spices, the tomato purée or passata, and the tomato paste. Turn down the heat to low and cook gently for 20 minutes. Add the water and simmer for 20 minutes, until the chicken is cooked.

Garnish with cilantro and serve with basmati rice.

Karahi ghosht

Mom used to make this dish on special occasions. It's one of my favorite dishes to serve to guests. Thick and flavorful, its rich spicy sauce is best mopped up with homemade roti (page 155), although you can also serve it with rice. It is also delicious with mango raita (page 167)

❁ Serves 4–6   ❁ Prep time: 20 mins   ❁ Cooking time: 60–90 mins

1 lb 10 oz (750 g) boneless lamb, beef, or venison (stewing cuts), cubed
¼ cup (60 ml) vegetable oil
1 tsp chopped green chili
1½ cups (350 g) tomato purée or passata

marinade
juice of ½ a lemon
2–3 garlic cloves, crushed
1 tsp grated fresh ginger
1 tsp salt
2 tsp Indian chili powder or cayenne
2 tsp ground coriander
1 tsp ground cumin
½ tsp garam masala

to garnish
1 green bell pepper, chopped or sliced into rings
1 onion, sliced into rings
1 large tomato, sliced into rounds

Make the marinade: In a large bowl, combine the lemon juice, garlic, ginger, and all the spices in a bowl and add the meat, mixing until it is well coated. Cover and refrigerate for at least 1 hour, but preferably overnight (the longer you leave it the better).

Heat the oil in a large pot, add the meat, along with its marinade, and cook, covered, on low heat for 45 minutes, checking from time to time to make sure it does not catch on the bottom of the pot.

Add the green chili and tomato purée or passata, and continue to cook over very low heat for another 20–30 minutes, until the meat is extremely tender.

Once ready, transfer to a large platter and garnish with the tomatoes, peppers, and onions. Serve with mango raita and roti.

Kofta with eggs

This is another favorite from my childhood. You can make the spicy Indian meatballs on their own or you can use the mixture to cover hard-boiled eggs, as I have done here. I make them both ways and they taste wonderful. Serve them with hot paratha (page 157).

Serves 6–8   Prep time: 30 mins   Cooking time: 40 mins

4 hard-boiled eggs, peeled and halved
1 tbsp butter
1 cup (240 g) plain yogurt
¼ tsp ground cumin
chopped cilantro, to garnish

kofta
1 lb (500 g) ground lamb, beef,
    or chicken
1 onion, finely chopped
1 egg
1 garlic clove, crushed
1 tsp ground coriander
½ tsp Indian chili powder or cayenne
½ tsp salt
¼ tsp turmeric
¼ tsp ground cumin
½ tsp garam masala
1 tsp green chili & cilantro paste
    (page 17)
1 slice of bread, moistened

sauce
1 tbsp vegetable oil
1 onion, finely sliced
1–2 garlic cloves, crushed
14 oz (400 g) can tomato purée
1 tsp ground coriander
1 tsp Indian chili powder or cayenne
½ tsp turmeric
½ tsp ground cumin
½ tsp salt
freshly ground black pepper

In a large bowl, mix all the kofta ingredients together well. Divide the mixture into 8 equal portions. Form each portion into a patty and place each patty on a piece of plastic wrap. Push an egg half down onto each patty (yolk side up) and pull up the sides of the plastic, forming a parcel. The egg should be completely encased in the meat, but this way your hands stay clean. Repeat with the remaining eggs and mixture and set aside.

In a large frying pan, heat the butter, yogurt, and cumin on low heat. Add the koftas, making sure they are well spaced in the pan. Cover and cook over low heat for 10–15 minutes until the meat has changed color, which means it is nearly cooked.

Meanwhile, make the sauce: Heat the oil in a medium pot with a lid. Add the onion and garlic. When they start to change color, add the tomato purée, then all the spices, salt, and pepper. Cover and simmer for 10–15 minutes on low heat, until the oil looks like it has separated.

Add the koftas and their cooking liquid to the pot, gently spooning over the tomato mixture until they are covered. Simmer on low heat for a further 5–10 minutes until the sauce thickenss slightly. Garnish with chopped cilantro and serve with hot paratha.

Chicken casserole with cassava

This is one of those hearty comfort foods that you can get cozy with beside the fireplace.
It is full of goodness—lots of vegetables, plus protein and a touch of spice.

❧ Serves 4–6   ❧ Prep time: 30 mins   ❧ Cooking time: 30 mins

1 lb (500 g) cassava (yuca), peeled
   and cut into chunks (frozen is fine)
2–3 tbsp vegetable oil
2 onions, sliced
1 boneless chicken breast, cubed
2 garlic cloves, crushed
½ tsp turmeric
¼ tsp ground cumin
½ tsp ground coriander
1 tsp Indian chili powder
   or cayenne
½ tsp paprika
1 tbsp tomato paste
3 tbsp tomato purée or passata
2 carrots, peeled and sliced
½ a cabbage, cut into chunks
½ cup (70 g) fresh or frozen peas
½ cup (45 g) broccoli florets
1⅔ cups (400 ml) water
salt

Place the pieces of cassava in a pot along with just enough water to cover it, and ½–1 teaspoon of salt. Bring to a boil and cook, uncovered, until tender, 15–20 minutes.

Meanwhile, in a large pot, heat the oil over medium heat and cook the sliced onions until translucent. Add the chicken and cook, stirring, for 5 minutes, then add 1 teaspoon of salt and the garlic and cook for a further 5–6 minutes until the chicken has changed color.

Add the turmeric, cumin, coriander, chili, paprika, tomato paste, and tomato purée or passata, stirring to make sure it is well combined. Then add all the vegetables, along with the measured water, and simmer on low heat until the chicken is cooked and the vegetables are tender, 20–30 minutes.

When the cassava is cooked, use a potato masher to mash it up in the water it was boiled in (pour out excess water if there is too much) to create a chunky, starchy mash. Remove any stringy stalks from the middle of the cassava as it breaks up.

Add the mash to the chicken and vegetables and stir well to mix. Serve immediately in bowls, with a crisp salad or some crusty bread alongside.

Spicy shepherd's pie

Mom was always good at adding a touch of spice to all her Western dishes. This is a great example—a traditional English shepherd's pie with a spicy twist.

Serves 4   Prep time: 15 mins   Cooking time: 30–40 mins

¼ cup (60 ml) vegetable oil
2 onions, sliced
1 lb (500 g) ground lamb or beef
1½ tsp ground coriander
1 tsp ground cumin
1 tsp paprika
¼ tsp turmeric
½ tsp Indian chili powder
  or cayenne
1 tsp salt
2–3 garlic cloves, crushed
1 tsp grated fresh ginger
14 oz (400 g) can diced tomatoes
  or tomato purée or passata
½ cup (70 g) fresh or frozen peas
½ cup (60 g) sliced carrots
6–8 potatoes, peeled and quartered
1 tsp butter
splash of milk
1 egg, beaten, for egg wash
mixed dried herbs, to garnish
  (optional)

Preheat the oven to 350F (180°C).

In a large sauté pan, heat the oil and fry the onion until golden. Add the ground meat, spices, salt, garlic, and ginger and cook, stirring, until the meat is browned. Add tomatoes, peas, and carrots and simmer for about 20 minutes. Set aside.

Boil the potatoes until soft. Drain and mash them with the butter and a splash of milk, making sure the mash is of a spreadable consistency.

Put the cooked meat into a 9 by 13 in (23 by 33 cm) baking dish, and evenly cover with the mashed potatoes. For a more decorative look, you can use a pastry bag to pipe on the mashed potatoes.

Brush the top with the beaten egg, sprinkle with dried herbs, if desired, and bake for 20–30 minutes until the top is golden. Serve hot.

Chana dhal

Dhal is the name of both the ingredient (split pulses) and the dish you make with them (a hearty thick soup). This is a classic dhal recipe, simple but full of flavor. There are so many varieties of dhal, it can get confusing. Chana dhal is a lovely dried yellow split chickpea, also known as split Bengal gram. Many dried legumes need soaking to reduce the cooking time, but since this dish is boiled, you can get away with not soaking them if you run out of time (just boil them for a little longer).

Serves 6–8   Prep time: 15 mins   Cooking time: 1 hour

dhal
2 cups (400 g) chana dhal (dried
   split chickpeas), rinsed and soaked
   in water overnight
½ cup (100 g) red lentils
1 tsp salt
1 tsp sugar

sauce
2 tbsp vegetable or coconut oil
1 small onion, sliced
2 medium green chili peppers
1 tsp salt
1 tsp ground coriander
1 tsp Indian chili powder
   or cayenne
1 tsp paprika
1 tsp crushed garlic
½ tsp ground cumin
½ tsp turmeric
scant 1 cup (200 g) tomato purée
   or passata
boiling water, if needed

In a pot, combine the chana dhal, lentils, salt, sugar, and 3–4 cups water. Bring to a boil, then simmer for 45 minutes, or until soft. Blend with a handheld immersion blender until you have a thick soup consistency. I like to leave some of the pulses whole to give the dish some texture.

In a frying pan, heat the oil and fry the onion until cooked and golden. Add the whole chilies, salt, spices, and tomato purée or passata. Bring to a simmer and cook over low heat for 5–7 minutes, until the oil separates.

Add the tomato mixture to the blended dhal and mix well, adding some boiling water if it is too thick. Allow to simmer over low heat for about 10 minutes until well combined, then serve with rice and fresh roti (page 155).

Spicy meatballs in yogurt

This is a great sharing plate or main dish if you are entertaining. The meatballs are especially good drizzled with yogurt and tamarind chutney (page 165) and fresh herbs. You could also sprinkle the dish with pomegranate seeds when they are in season.

Serves 4–6   Prep time: 30 mins   Cooking time: 20 mins

1 lb (500 g) ground beef
1½ cups (75 g) dried breadcrumbs
1 onion, finely chopped
2 fresh green chilies,
    finely chopped
1 in (3 cm) fresh ginger, grated
2 tsp ground coriander
1 egg, beaten
salt and freshly ground black
    pepper
vegetable oil, for frying

to serve
1–2 cups (240–500 g) plain yogurt,
    to serve
tamarind chutney (page 165)
2–3 tbsp chopped fresh cilantro
Indian chili powder or cayenne
fresh pomegranate seeds (optional)

In a large bowl, mix the ground beef, breadcrumbs, onion, chilies, ginger, coriander, beaten egg, salt, and pepper. Ensure the mixture is combined well. Using the palm of your hand, shape the mixture into small balls, about 1½ in (4 cm) in diameter.

Coat the bottom of a frying pan with oil and place over medium heat. Working in batches, fry the meatballs until cooked and brown on all sides, 6–8 minutes. Using a slotted spoon, transfer to a plate lined with paper towels to drain excess oil.

Transfer the meatballs to a serving dish, and spoon the yogurt and tamarind chutney over them. Garnish with cilantro and chili powder, and sprinkle with pomegrante seeds, if using. Serve warm.

Fish & coconut curry

This fragrant curry is quick and easy; perfect for a midweek meal. You can use any firm white fish for this recipe.

❀ Serves 4–6   ❀ Prep time: 20 mins   ❀ Cooking time: 25 mins

1 tbsp vegetable oil
½ tsp mustard seeds
1 onion, diced
1 green bell pepper, thinly sliced
1 garlic clove, crushed
1 tbsp curry powder
¼ tsp turmeric
scant 1 cup (200 g) canned tomato
  purée or passata
2 firm white fish fillets, such as
  snapper or sea bass, cut into
  1½ in (4 cm) cubes
scant 1 cup (200 ml) coconut milk
salt

Heat the oil in a large sauté pan over medium–high heat, add the mustard seeds, and cook until they start to pop. Add the onion, green pepper, and garlic, and fry, stirring, for 2 minutes.

Add the curry powder and turmeric, and continue to cook on low heat for 5 minutes. Then add the puréed tomatoes and the fish, and simmer until fish is opaque, 10–15 minutes.

Gently stir in the coconut milk and bring to a simmer to heat through. Taste and season with salt to your liking. Serve with basmati rice.

Garlic & green pepper chicken curry

This lovely, authentic curry is full of flavor, and perfect for dinner parties or special occasions, but it is also quick and easy to make. The green pepper gives it a lovely crunch and the garlic brings the flavors together. Serve it with vegetable pulau (page 138).

 Serves 4–6   Prep time: 1 hour   Cooking time: 35 mins

2 green chilies, deseeded and
　chopped
3 garlic cloves, crushed
small piece fresh ginger, grated
3 tsp ground cumin
1 tsp salt
1 large onion, coarsely chopped
1 tbsp white vinegar
2 boneless chicken breasts, cubed
3 tbsp ghee or vegetable oil
2 green bell peppers, sliced
½ tsp freshly ground black pepper
juice of 1 lemon

In a food processor or using a mortar and pestle, blend the chilies, garlic, ginger, cumin, salt, onion, and vinegar to a paste. Transfer to a bowl, add the chicken, and mix well to coat. Refrigerate for 1 hour to marinate.

Heat the ghee or oil in a frying pan, add the chicken with its marinade, cover, and cook over low heat for 20–25 minutes.

Add the sliced peppers and fry, uncovered, for an additional 10 minutes, until the chicken and peppers are cooked.

Sprinkle with black pepper and lemon juice and serve with vegetable pulau.

Mung dhal

Growing up. this was our usual Sunday brunch. Our tradition was to serve it with fried eggs and hot roti drizzled with melted ghee. Mung dhal (dried split mung beans) is pale yellow in color but you can also use orange-red lentils, which are similar in shape and size.

 Serves 4—6   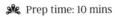 Prep time: 10 mins   Cooking time: 20—30 mins

2 cups (400 g) mung dhal (dried
   split mung beans), rinsed and
   soaked overnight in cold water
2 tbsp vegetable oil
1—2 small whole green chilies
   (optional)
1 tsp salt
½ tsp crushed garlic
1 tsp ground coriander
1 tsp Indian chili powder
   or cayenne
1 tsp paprika
¼ tsp ground cumin
¼ tsp turmeric
scant 1 cup (200 g) tomato purée
   or passata
chopped fresh cilantro,
   for garnish

Drain and rinse the dhal. In a pot, heat the oil over medium heat and fry the whole chilies for 3 minutes, then add the mung dhal.

Stirring continuously, add the salt, garlic, and all of the spices and cook for 3 minutes, then add the tomato purée or passata. Turn down the heat to low, and cook, still stirring, for 5 minutes, then add about 1 cup (240 ml) of water (more if you want it really soft). Simmer over low heat for about 15 minutes. The consistency is a personal preference; I like mine like a thick soup.

Once cooked to your desired consistency, garnish with cilantro and serve with fresh roti (page 155).

Akni

Akni (curried rice) is traditionally served at Memon weddings, and cooked in a "deg," a very large pot for mass cooking. Weddings were always a big affair when I was growing up in Malawi, and this dish, along with sweet rice with raisins and cherries (page 146), would be cooked in huge quantities by the older women of the Memon community. These traditions have long gone, but the beautiful dishes remain.

Serves 6–8   Prep time: 20 mins   Cooking time: 40–60 mins

for the meat
½ cup (120 ml) vegetable oil
1 large onion, sliced
1 tsp whole cumin seeds
1 cinnamon stick
2–3 cardamom pods
2 cloves
4 whole peppercorns
1 tsp turmeric
1½ tsp crushed garlic
1½ tsp grated ginger
2½ tsp salt
¾ tsp freshly ground black pepper
2¼ lb (1 kg) boneless lamb shoulder
  or bone-in chicken pieces,
  skin removed
6 potatoes, quartered
14 oz (400 g) can tomato purée
  or passata
3 tbsp tomato paste
chopped cilantro, to garnish

second set of spices
3 tsp ground coriander
2 tsp ground cumin
2 tsp Indian chili powder or cayenne
1 tsp paprika

rice
2½ cups (500 g) basmati rice, rinsed
5 cups (1.2 liters) boiling water
2 tbsp ghee or butter

In a large pot, heat the oil over medium heat and fry the onion with the spices, garlic, ginger, salt, and pepper. When the onion is soft and golden, add the chicken or lamb and the potatoes, turn down the heat to low, and cook, covered, for 10 minutes, stirring once so they don't stick.

Stir in the tomato purée or passata and tomato paste. Re-cover, and continue to cook on low heat for 10 minutes for chicken, or 20 minutes for lamb, then mix in the second set of spices. Continue to cook, covered, until the meat and potatoes are tender and the sauce has thickened and clings to the meat, about 10 more minutes for chicken, or 20 more minutes for lamb.

Next, add the rice, boiling water, and ghee, stir, cover the pot, and simmer on the lowest heat setting until the rice is cooked and the liquid has been absorbed, 18–20 minutes.

Transfer to a serving platter, garnish with some fresh cilantro, and serve with sweet rice with raisins and cherries (page 146).

On the side

You can't have an Indian meal without perfect rice or buttery naan to mop up your spicy sauces, and some sweet-and-sour chutneys to accompany them. This section also has a step-by-step guide to making traditional Indian breads.

Dad's basmati rice

I think this recipe is an absolute winner. My dad, Hamid, has been making rice this way for as long as I can remember. Dad is a perfectionist and very methodical—the complete opposite of my mom—and even though he doesn't cook much, being in the kitchen with him is always a pleasure.

Serves 4—6   Prep time: 10 mins   Cooking time: 15 mins

2½ cups (500 g) basmati rice
1 tbsp butter
1 tbsp olive oil
1 onion, finely sliced
5 cups (1.2 liters) boiling water
2 tsp salt
fried or grilled whole chilies, to
   garnish (optional)

Rinse the rice in a bowl a couple of times, draining all of the water away, then soak the rice in cold water for at least 30 minutes, but ideally for a couple of hours.

In a heavy-based pot with a lid, heat the butter and oil over medium—low heat, and sauté the onion until pale golden.

Add the drained rice, stirring with a wooden spoon until it starts to look translucent and sticks to the base of the pot, 3—4 minutes.

Add the boiling water, then the salt. Return to a boil, then reduce heat to the lowest setting and cover the pot. Simmer gently for 15—20 minutes until all the water has been absorbed and the rice is cooked. Make sure that the heat is really low or it will stick to the bottom of the pot and burn. The rice should be fluffy and the grains separate, not sticking together.

Serve with any meat dish or curry.

Vegetable pulau

This is a lovely dish to have on its own or makes for a colorful addition to meat dishes. It is easy and versatile and you add whatever vegetables you have on hand. My mom always cooked this dish for meat-free days, served with the delicious spicy peppers in tomato sauce (page 72).

✤ Serves 4   ✤ Prep time: 20 mins   ✤ Cooking time: 15 mins

1 tbsp vegetable oil
1 onion, finely sliced
½ tsp cumin seeds
small piece of cinnamon stick
1–2 cardamom pods
1–2 cloves crushed garlic
1 tsp green chili & cilantro paste
   (page 17)
½ tsp ground cumin
1 cup mixed fresh or frozen
   vegetables, such as cauliflower
   florets, peas, beans, corn,
   diced bell peppers, etc
1 potato or sweet potato, peeled and
   diced (optional, for a heartier dish)
1½ cups (300 g) basmati rice,
   soaked in cold water for
   30 minutes, rinsed, and drained
3 cups (700 ml) boiling water
1½ tsp salt

In a large saucepan, heat the oil over medium heat, and sauté the onion until translucent. Add the whole spices and cook, stirring, for 2 minutes, then add the garlic, chili & cilantro paste, and ground cumin. Mix well, and cook for an additional 3 minutes.

Add all of the vegetables and cook, stirring, for 3–5 minutes.

Add the rice, along with the boiling water and salt. Return to a bubbling boil, then reduce the heat to its lowest setting, cover the pot, and simmer gently for 15–20 minutes until all the water has been absorbed and the rice is cooked.

Fluff with a fork before serving.

Kitchrie

This is a staple dish in my family. It is one of those comfort foods that brings back memories of winter in the UK and sitting by the fire. Kitchrie goes well with chundo (ground lamb curry) and dollops of currie (page 106). Just divine.

Serves 4—6   Prep time: 10 mins   Cooking time: 15—20 mins

2 cups (400 g) basmati rice, rinsed
¼ cup (50 g) split black gram or
   split green urad dhal, rinsed
1 tbsp vegetable oil
4 cups (1 liter) boiling water
1 tsp salt
1 tbsp ghee or butter, cut into pieces

Soak the rice and dhal together in cold water for at least 30 minutes. Rinse under cold running water until the water drains clear. Set aside.

In a large lidded pot, heat the oil over medium heat and add the rice and dhal. Cook, stirring, for a couple of minutes until the rice starts to stick to the pan, then add the water and salt.

Return to a bubbling boil, then reduce the heat to its lowest setting, cover the pot, and simmer gently for 15—20 minutes until the water has been absorbed and the rice and dhal are cooked.

Turn off the heat. Add the ghee or butter to the kitchrie and stir really well with a wooden spoon. Unlike many other rice dishes, this is better soft and a little mushy, rather than fluffy and separated. Serve hot.

Şaffron rice

Rice and saffron is a heavenly combination. This is not the simplest way to cook rice, but really worth the effort for special occasions. This rice dish is perfect to impress your guests at a dinner party or for a celebration.

Serves 4—6   Prep time: 10 mins   Cooking time: 15 mins

½ tsp saffron threads, plus extra
  to garnish
3 cups (700 ml) boiling water,
  plus 1 tbsp extra
3 tbsp ghee or vegetable oil
2 onions, sliced
3—4 whole cloves
2—3 whole cardamom pods
1½ tsp salt
1 tsp freshly ground black pepper
1½ cups (300 g) basmati rice,
  thoroughly rinsed and drained
edible gold or silver leaf, to garnish
  (optional)

In a small bowl, soak the saffron threads in 1 tablespoon of boiling water for 30 minutes.

Heat the ghee or oil in a large pot, add the onions, and fry gently for 4—5 minutes until soft and pale.

Add the whole spices, salt, and black pepper and cook for 2 minutes, then add the rice. Fry together for 3 minutes, stirring frequently, until the rice starts to stick to the pot.

Pour in the boiling water, along with the saffron and its soaking liquid. Return to a boil, then reduce the heat to its lowest setting, cover the pot, and simmer gently for 15—20 minutes until the water has been absorbed and the rice is cooked.

Transfer the rice to a serving dish and garnish with saffron threads and and pieces of gold or silver leaf, if you wish.

Turmeric rice

This variation on simple cooked rice will enhance any curry to the next level. It's a favorite of my children, especially my son, Adam. The turmeric adds a subtle flavor that makes all the difference. I serve it at least once a week with curry.

❧ Serves 4–6   ❧ Prep time: 15 mins   ❧ Cooking time: 15 mins

2 tbsp vegetable oil, plus extra
  for frying
2 cups (400 g) basmati rice,
  soaked in cold water for at least
  30 minutes and drained
4 cups (1 liter) boiling water
2 tsp salt
¼ tsp turmeric
1 onion, finely sliced

In a pot, heat the 2 tablespoons oil over medium heat and add the drained rice. Cook for 2 minutes, stirring to ensuring the rice doesn't stick to the bottom of the pan. Add the boiling water, salt, and turmeric and return to a boil. Reduce the heat to its lowest setting, cover the pot, and simmer gently for 15–20 minutes until the water has been absorbed and the rice is cooked.

Pour enough oil into a large frying pan to coat the base and fry the onion until golden and crispy. Set aside on a plate lined with paper towels to drain excess oil and crisp up.

Serve the rice, garnished with the onions, alongside your favorite curry.

Sweet rice with raisins & cherries

Traditionally this dish is served with akni (curried rice, page 131) during Memon weddings. It is the epitome of my heritage and brings back memories of growing up in Memon communities in Malawi and the UK. Cherries are traditional, but you can also use pineapple.

serves 4–6   Prep time: 10 mins   Cooking time: 15 mins

1 cup (200 g) basmati rice, soaked in cold water for at least 30 minutes
1 tbsp vegetable oil
2 cups (480 ml) boiling water
drop of orange food coloring
½ cup (100 g) sugar
¼ cup (40 g) raisins
¼ cup (80 g) halved cherries or chopped pineapple (fresh or canned)

Rinse the rice under cold running water until it runs clear. Drain well.

In a pot, heat the oil over medium heat and add the rice. Cook, stirring, for 2–3 minutes until it starts to stick to the pot. Add the boiling water and food coloring.

Return to a boil, then lower the heat, cover the pot, and simmer until the water is nearly absorbed, 12–14 minutes.

Stir in the sugar and fruits and replace the lid. Gently cook the mixture over low heat for a further 10 minutes, until the rice is cooked and all the water has been absorbed.

Cassava fries

This is one of my childhood favorites. We often had these as a snack, sprinkled with salt and chili powder. They also make a great side for dishes like my chili-basted roast chicken (page 85). Cassava (yuka) is available from South Asian and Latin American specialty stores and some supermarkets.

❧ Serves 4—6   **❧ Prep time: 25 mins**   **❧ Cooking time: 45 mins**

1 lb 5 oz (600 g) fresh or frozen
    cassava (yuka), peeled and cut
    into large pieces
salt
1 egg, beaten (optional)
vegetable oil, for frying
Indian chili powder or cayenne,
    to garnish

Place the cassava in a pot of salted boiling water and cook until soft, 15—20 minutes.

Drain, cool, and remove the stalk from the middle, then cut into evenly sized chunky fries. If you like, coat them in the beaten egg, which will give them texture.

Pour the oil into a heavy-based pot to a depth of 2 in (5 cm). Heat until the surface shimmers and a small piece of bread turns golden. Working in batches, fry the cassava fries in oil for 6—8 minutes, turning from time to time, until golden on all sides.

Using a slotted spoon, transfer the fries to a plate lined with paper towels to drain excess oil. Season to taste with salt and chili powder.

Ănjum's spicy roast potatoes

These roast potatoes are so divine, and my sister's specialty. They go perfectly with any roasted dinner, and add a touch of spice to your meal. Try them with chili-crusted baked salmon (page 80) or roast lamb with a chili rub (page 98), and cucumber raita (page 167) on the side.

❧ Serves 8   ❧ Prep time: 15 mins   ❧ Cooking time: 45–50 mins

8–10 large potatoes, peeled and cut into slices about ½ in (1.5 cm) thick
½ cup (120 ml) vegetable oil
1–2 tsp Indian chili powder or cayenne
1 tsp paprika
1 tsp salt, plus extra as needed
½ tsp freshly ground black pepper
2 tsp white vinegar
2 tbsp ketchup
1–2 garlic cloves, crushed

to garnish
crushed red pepper flakes
lemon wedges, grilled if desired

Preheat the oven to 320°F (160°C).

In a large pot of salted water, parboil the potatoes for 6–8 minutes until softened but not breakable.

In a bowl, mix the oil, chili powder, paprika, salt, pepper, vinegar, ketchup, and garlic.

Line a baking pan with foil, brush the foil with the chili oil mixture, and then spread the sliced potatoes over the pan, turning to make sure they are all well-coated in chili oil.

Bake for 30 minutes, turning the potatoes halfway through so they cook evenly.

Garnish with chili flakes and a squeeze of lemon, and serve with cucumber raita (page 167).

Naan

Naan is a delicious, puffy Indian bread made with milk and yogurt, traditionally cooked on the walls of a tandoor (clay oven). It is not easy to recreate this intense heat at home, but this version, cooked under the broiler, still tastes divine. It is perfect for mopping up curries or eating on its own.

❧ Makes 6–8   ❧ Prep time: 30 mins   ❧ Cooking time: 30 mins

3 cups (360 g) all-purpose flour
1½ tsp sugar
½ tsp salt
1 tsp baking powder
½ tsp baking soda
¼ cup (60 ml) milk
⅓ cup (80 ml) plain yogurt
1 tbsp butter, melted, plus
    extra for brushing
¾ cup (180 ml) warm water,
    or as needed

Optional toppings
poppyseeds
chopped fresh cilantro
cumin seeds
chopped fresh mint
crushed red pepper flakes

Sift the flour into a large bowland mix in the sugar, salt, baking powder, and baking soda. Make a well in the center and add the milk, yogurt, melted butter, and warm water. Mix until it comes together into a dough.

On a lightly floured work surface, knead the dough until smooth, 6–8 minutes. Divide into 6–8 balls. Roll out into oblong naan shapes, each about 2 in (5 cm) thick.

Turn on your broiler.

Heat a dry nonstick frying pan over medium heat, and cook each naan on one side for 2 minutes until golden, and then place on a baking pan, cooked side down. Brush the top with melted butter, and sprinkle with any toppings you choose.

Working in batches if needed, cook under the broiler until browned, blistered, and cooked through. This usually takes about 2 minutes, but watch carefully.

Best eaten on the day they are made, but you can store leftovers in foil for an additional day or so.

Roti

A staple in any Indian home, we tend to eat these simple wholewheat flatbreads with everything. Roti is perfect with curries, eggs, or on its own with a cup of tea. I grew up eating roti hot from the pan, smeared with ghee, sprinkled with sugar, and rolled up. Nowadays, whenever I make roti, my children emerge to ask for a sugar roti.

Makes 10–12   Prep time: 30–40 mins   Cooking time: 30 mins

3 cups (360 g) all-purpose or chapati flour (or 2 cups/240 g all-purpose + 1 cup/120 g wholewheat flour), plus extra for dusting
½ tsp salt (optional)
1 tbsp melted ghee or butter, plus extra for brushing
1 cup (240 ml) warm water

Sift the flour and salt into a large bowl. Make a well in the center and add the melted butter or ghee, then slowly mix in the warm water until it forms a dough. Turn out onto a lightly floured surface and knead for 8–10 minutes until soft and pliable. Place in a bowl, cover with a damp cloth, and set aside for 20 minutes.

Return the dough to your floured work surface and divide it into 10–12 equal portions, depending on your preferred size. Using your hands, flatten each portion into a disc about 2 in (5 cm) in diameter. Use your finger to make a small impression in the center. Smear this with a little melted butter or ghee and sprinkle some all-purpose flour on top. Pinch the dough over the ghee or butter to make a parcel and then roll it into a ball, setting it aside under a damp cloth until you have done all of them.

Lightly flour your rolling pin—I use an Indian rolling pin that is thin and tapered towards the ends—and roll out each ball to a thin round about 6 in (15 cm) in diameter, turning the dough at ¼-circle intervals to get an even thickness. You can dust with more flour while rolling, but remember to remove excess flour at the end (place the roti in the palm of your hand and gently slap it from one hand to the other).

Place a nonstick frying pan, flat griddle pan, or a tava/tawri (an Indian chapati pan) if you have one over medium–high heat until hot. Place a roti on the hot pan for 10 seconds or until bubbles form on the underside, then turn the roti using a spatula and press down as you cook the other side (this will make the roti puff up). Turn once more, pressing down again. Once cooked (each roti shouldn't take more than 30–40 seconds in total), brush the roti with melted ghee or butter and stack on a plate, covered with a tea towel while you cook the rest. Best eaten hot.

Paratha

These fried Indian breads are delicious. We don't make them as often as roti because they are fried in butter or ghee, so we save them for special occasions. They are heavier than roti, flaky, and crispy and one is often enough, especially if you are filling it. You can serve these as an accompaniment to rice and curry dishes or have them for lunch.

❧ Makes 8–10   ❧ Prep time: 40 mins   ❧ Cooking time: 30 mins

3 cups (360 g) all-purpose or chapati flour (or 2 cups/120 g all-purpose + 1 cup/240 g wholewheat flour), plus extra for dusting
½ tsp salt (optional)
½ cup (120 g) ghee or butter, melted
1 cup (240 ml) warm water

potential flavorings
½ tsp whole cumin seeds mixed with ¼ tsp ground coriander; OR ¾ tsp dukkah and a pinch of crushed red pepper flakes

mashed potato filling (optional)
3–4 small potatoes, boiled and mashed with ½ tsp Kashmiri chili powder, a squeeze of lemon juice, 1 tbsp of chopped fresh cilantro or spinach, and salt to taste

Sift the flour and salt into a large bowl. Make a well in the center and add 1 tablespoon of melted ghee or butter, then slowly mix in the warm water until it forms a dough. Turn out onto a lightly floured surface and knead for 8–10 minutes until you have a soft, pliable dough. Place in a bowl, cover with a damp cloth, and set aside for 20 minutes.

On a lightly floured surface, divide the dough into 8–10 portions, roll each portion out into a thin round 6–7 in (15–18 cm) in diameter. Brush the entire surface with about a teaspoon of melted butter or ghee (at this point you can sprinkle on one of the suggested flavorings or add a thin layer of mashed potato filling— too much and the dough won't roll smoothly and the filling will spill out.) Tightly roll the dough round into a log (a little bit like a Swiss roll) and repeat with the rest of the rounds.

Coil each log into a tight round, flatten with your palm and, dusting with flour as you go, roll out again into a circle 6–7 in (15–18 cm) in diameter.

Heat a nonstick frying pan or flat griddle pan over medium–high heat and add about ½ teaspoon of melted butter or ghee. Place a paratha on the hot pan and cook for about 10 seconds, until it starts to turn golden. Use a spatula to turn it over and drizzle another ½ teaspoon of melted butter or ghee around the edges, tipping the pan so it is evenly distributed. Turn over again and cook until it's golden and crispy, about 1½ minutes. Set aside, covered with foil or in a warm oven until you have cooked them all.

Puri

These are so simple, and one of my favorite things to make with my children. Forming the dough is a fun way to get the kids involved, with lots of laughter and lots of mess. Bliss! Puris can be served alongside curries, or with a sweet filling, such as kheeraj (page 180), or a savory filling, such as pani puri (page 33).

Makes 10–12   Prep time: 20 mins   Cooking time: 20–30 mins

1 cup (120 g) all-purpose flour
¼ tsp baking powder
¼ tsp salt
1 tbsp vegetable oil, plus
  extra for frying
½ cup (120 ml) cold water,
  as needed

In a large bowl, combine the flour, baking powder, salt, and 1 tablespoon of vegetable oil. Mix well. Gradually mix in just enough of the cold water to form a soft dough (you may not use it all).

On a lightly floured surface, divide the dough into 10–12 pieces and roll into balls. Form each ball into a round about 4 in (10 cm) in diameter.

Pour the oil into a heavy-based pot to a depth of 2 in (5 cm). Heat until the surface shimmers and a small piece of the dough turns golden. Working in small batches, fry the puris for 1–1½ minutes, spooning hot oil over them as you go (this is what will achieve the hollow inside), until they are golden and puffed up.

Using a slotted spoon, transfer the puris to a plate lined with paper towels to drain excess oil.

1. **Tamarillo chutney**
2. **Date & tomato chutney**
3. **Mango chutney**
4. **Tamarind chutney**
5. **Cilantro chutney**
6. **Apple chutney**
7. **Tomato chutney**

4

Apple chutney

My mom began making this recipe when we lived in the UK. We had a small apple tree in the backyard, laden with tart apples that worked well in a chutney. It's a perfect accompaniment to any Indian appetizer.

🌿 Makes approx. 4 cups (1 liter)
🌿 Prep time: 15 mins
🌿 Cooking time: 70 mins

syrup
2½ cups (500 g) sugar
1½ cups (350 ml) water

chutney
¼ cup (40 g) raisins or golden raisins
4 tbsp Indian chili powder, or 2 tbsp cayenne
1 tbsp salt
4–6 garlic cloves, peeled and crushed
5 lb (2.25 kg) apples, peeled, cored, and diced
    (I like to use Braeburn)
3 cups (750 ml) apple cider vinegar

In a small pot, combine the sugar and water and bring to a boil. Turn down the heat and simmer until it's of a syrup consistency, 6–8 minutes.

Using a food processor or handheld immersion blender, blend the raisins, chili powder, salt, and garlic to a paste. Set aside.

In a large heavy-based pot, combine the apples and vinegar and boil, uncovered, for about 45 minutes, until the apples are soft. Add the raisin paste and the syrup and continue to boil gently for 20 minutes, until thick enough to coat the back of a spoon.

Allow to cool. Transfer to jars and store in the refrigerator for up to 1 month.

Tomato chutney or Cilantro chutney

These two quick chutneys are so lovely and versatile. Serve them with your favorite curry or appetizer. I especially love the tomato chutney with curried chicken and pea pastries (page 45).

🌿 Makes 1–1¼ cups (240–300 ml)
🌿 Prep time: 10 mins

tomato chutney
1 bunch fresh cilantro, stalks removed
1 large tomato
2–3 green chilies (less if you prefer)
juice of ½ a lemon
1 tsp salt, or to taste
2 tbsp ketchup
1–2 tsp Indian chili powder
    or cayenne
½ tsp brown sugar

cilantro chutney
1 bunch fresh cilantro, stalks removed
2–3 green chilies
2 tbsp lemon juice
small handful mint leaves
pinch of sugar, or to taste
salt and freshly ground black pepper

To make either chutney, use a food processor or a handheld immersion blender to blend all the ingredients together into a coarse paste. Taste to make sure it is seasoned to your liking.

Transfer to a jar or container. Both chutneys can be stored in the refrigerator for up to 4 days.

Mango chutney

Homemade mango chutney will bring your Indian meal to the next level. The delicate flavor of golden mangoes shine through the complexity of spices. It's easier to make than you think and is perfect with cheeses and charcuterie, as well as any curry.

- Makes 1⅔ cups (400 ml)
- Prep time: 10 mins
- Cooking time: 15 mins

2 large mangoes, peeled, pitted, and diced
2 tbsp lime juice
2 tbsp vegetable oil
½–1 tsp crushed red pepper flakes
1 tsp cumin seeds
½–1 tsp coriander seeds
½ tsp mustard seeds
3–4 tbsp brown sugar
¾ cup (180 ml) white wine vinegar
salt and freshly ground black pepper

Place the mangoes in a bowl and squeeze the lime juice over them. Toss and set aside.

In a medium pot, heat the oil over medium heat and add the spices. Stir for a few seconds, then add the sugar and vinegar. Turn down the heat and simmer, uncovered, for 7 minutes.

Add the mango, season with salt and pepper, and continue to cook for a further 7–8 minutes until the mango is silky and the liquid becomes syrupy. Allow to cool.

Transfer to jars and store in the refrigerator for up to 1 week. Serve at room temperature.

Date & tomato chutney

An easy chutney to impress your family and friends, this goes perfectly with any of the delicious morsels in the "Grazing & Bites" section, or simply with cheese and crackers. Traditionally chutneys are always used as a dip for samosas and bhajias.

- Makes approx. 4 cups (1 liter)
- Prep time: 15 mins
- Cooking time: 45 mins

9 oz (250 g) pitted dates, coarsely chopped
14 oz (400 g) can diced tomatoes
1 onion, finely diced
1½ in (4 cm) piece of fresh ginger, peeled and chopped
1 tsp Indian chili powder or cayenne
1 tsp salt
6 tbsp cider or malt vinegar

In a medium pot, combine all of the ingredients together and mix well. Bring to a boil and then turn down the heat and simmer, uncovered, for 45 minutes until thickened. Allow to cool.

Transfer to jars and store in the refrigerator for up to 1 month.

Tamarillo chutney

This is the first chutney I ever made. It is my absolute favorite, and the inspiration for the name of my first blog. Tamarillos are are a sweet, tomato-like fruit native to Central and South America. They are brazenly beautiful, glossy, and smooth, and they are divine in chutneys or cooked in desserts. This recipe was given to me by my "Kiwi mom," Marion Robertson.

- Makes 4 cups (1 liter)
- Prep time: 30 mins
- Cooking time: 1–1½ hours

2¾ lb (1.25 kg) tamarillos
9 oz (250 g) cooking apples, peeled, cored, and diced
1 lb (500 g) onions, diced
1 cups (250 ml) apple cider vinegar
2⅓ cups (500 g) brown sugar
½ tsp salt
½ tsp cayenne pepper (optional)

Dip the tamarillos briefly in a pot of boiling water to loosen their skins. Once cooled slightly, peel them, then coarsely chop.

Place the chopped tamarillos in a heavy-based pot, along with the all of the other ingredients. Bring to a boil, then turn down the heat and simmer gently for 1–1½ hours, stirring occasionally, until the mixture is thick and syrupy. Allow to cool.

Transfer to jars and store in the refrigerator for up to 1 month.

Tamarind chutney

This is a really quick and easy chutney. It is used in India like ketchup is used in the West. Tamarind chutney goes with everything and adds a tangy, sweet-and-sour flavor with a touch of spice. Tamarind paste and fresh tamarind are available in Indian supermarkets. This chutney goes well with a great number of dishes, for example pani puri (page 33).

- Makes approx. ½ cup (120 ml)
- Prep time: 5 mins
- Cooking time: 10 mins

2 tsp tamarind pulp or purée
3–4 tsp brown sugar
¼ tsp salt
¼ tsp freshly ground black pepper
1 tsp cumin seeds, lightly toasted
6–8 tbsp water

In a small heavy-based pot, combine all of the ingredients and bring to a boil. Turn down the heat and simmer for a few minutes until you have a syrupy liquid. If it gets too thick, just add an additional tablespoon or two of boiling water. Allow to cool.

Transfer to a small jar or container and store in the refrigerator for up to 1 month.

Cucumber raita or Mango raita

Raita is a staple in Indian homes—everyone has their own version. You can choose to use plain or thicker Greek yogurt.

- Makes 1–2 cups (240–500 ml)
- Prep time: 10 mins
- Cooking time: 5 mins

cucumber raita
1⅔ cups (400 g) plain or Greek yogurt
½ cup (50 g) diced cucumber,
  plus extra to garnish
1 tbsp chopped fresh cilantro,
  plus extra to garnish
½ tbsp chopped fresh mint
salt and freshly ground black pepper
sprinkle of Indian chili powder (optional)

mango raita
2 mangoes, peeled, pitted, and finely diced
1⅔ cups (400 g) plain yogurt
1 tbsp dried shredded coconut
1 tsp sugar
salt and freshly ground black pepper
¼ cup (5 g) chopped cilantro
1 tsp vegetable oil
¼ tsp mustard seeds
¼ tsp crushed red pepper flakes

For the cucumber raita: Mix all ingredients together. Spoon into a serving bowl, and garnish as desired.

For the mango raita: In a bowl, combine the mangoes (reserving a handful to garnish), yogurt, coconut, sugar, and some salt and pepper. Mix in the cilantro. Sprinkle with the reserved mango. Heat the oil in a small frying pan and fry the spices until the seeds start popping. Let cool, and pour over the raita.

Best eaten on the day, or covered and refrigerated for 1 more day.

Tomato & onion relish

This quick and easy relish is perfect to serve with any curry or rice dish. The chili adds the spicy, tangy flavor and the onions add texture.

- Makes 1–1¼ cups (240–300 ml)
- Prep time: 5 mins

1 large tomato, diced
1 onion, diced or sliced
1 scallion, sliced
½ tsp Indian chili powder
  or cayenne
¼ tsp salt
dash of white vinegar

Simply mix all of the ingredients together. Serve on the day it is made, as an accompaniment to curry and rice dishes.

A touch of sweetness

"Desserts are like songs—the best ones make you dance." This sums up the following recipes for me. Traditional Indian sweets are typically sweet and decadent, but you can also elevate a wide variety of desserts to a whole new level with Indian spices like cardamom, saffron, and cinnamon. This section includes some of my favorite desserts, both traditional and adapted, like refreshing mango kulfi (ice cream), pavlova flavored with rose and pistachios, cardamom shortbread cookies, and carrot halva. Your senses are in for a treat!

Carrot halva with mascarpone

Halva is a dense, sweet category of dessert. Indian desserts can be sweet and decadent, and this carrot halva is no exception—sticky and gorgeous. It is decadent enough for a celebration, but very easy to make. We served it at my sister Nishat's wedding, decorated with edible flowers.

❧ Serves 4   ❧ Prep time: 20 mins   ❧ Cooking time: 50 mins

5 cups (1.2 liters) whole milk
9 oz (250 g) carrots, peeled
  and grated
¼ tsp ground cardamom (optional)
5 tbsp (75 g) butter
scant 1 cup (175 g) sugar
¼ cup (40 g) raisins (optional)

to serve
mascarpone, whipped cream,
  or Greek yogurt
handful of chopped pistachios
edible flowers (optional)

In a heavy-based pot, combine the milk, carrots, and cardamom, if using. Place over medium–high heat and cook, stirring occasionally with a wooden spoon, until the liquid has evaporated, 25–30 minutes. Keep an eye on it—you don't want it to catch on the bottom.

Add the butter, sugar, and raisins (if using), and stir until the butter has melted and the sugar has dissolved.

Let it cook for an additional 10–15 minutes, stirring frequently, until the mixture starts to come away from the side of the pot.

Transfer to four small (¼-cup/60 ml capacity) ramekins or molds.

Let the mixture cool a little, then turn out onto plates and serve with a dollop of mascarpone, whipped cream, or yogurt. a sprinkle of chopped pistachios, and edible flowers, if desired.

Serve warm or at room temperature.

Beet halva

A friend suggested I try making a beet halva and I'm so pleased she did. The flavor is rich and sweet, and the color is simply stunning. Garnish with some lovely edible flowers and serve with mascarpone, whipped cream, or Greek yogurt.

❀ Serves 4   ❀ Prep time: 20 mins   ❀ Cooking time: 50–60 mins

5 cups (1.2 liters) whole milk
7 oz (200 g) beets, peeled and grated
3–4 cardamom pods
5 tbsp (75 g) butter
¾ cup (150 g) sugar
whipped cream, Greek yogurt
  or mascarpone, to serve
edible flowers, to garnish (optional)

In a heavy-based pot, combine the milk and beets. Place over high heat and cook, stirring occasionally with a wooden spoon, until the liquid has evaporated, about 30 minutes. Watch carefully—you don't want it to catch on the bottom.

Crush the cardamom pods and extract the black seeds. Grind the seeds to a powder using a mortar and pestle.

Add the butter, sugar, and cardamom to the pot and stir until the butter has melted and the sugar has dissolved.

Cook a further 15–20 minutes, stirring frequently, until the mixture starts to come away from the side of the pan.

Transfer to individual serving bowls and serve with a dollop of whipped cream, Greek yogurt, or mascarpone and a garnish of edible flowers. Serve warm or at room temperature.

Sticky date cake with caramel sauce

This is my sister Farha's go-to dessert for entertaining and it makes a tasty finish to an Indian meal. The cake is divine, rich, and oozing with flavor, and topped with a luscious caramel sauce. This recipe can be made ahead of time and heated up before serving.

❋ Serves 6   ❋ Prep time: 20 mins   ❋ Cooking time: 40 mins

6 oz (170 g) pitted dates, chopped
scant ¾ cup (170 ml) boiling water
½ tsp vanilla extract
2 tsp unsweetened cocoa powder
¾ tsp baking soda
7 tbsp (100 g) butter, softened, plus
   extra for greasing
¾ cup (150 g) sugar
2 eggs, lightly beaten
1½ cups (170 g) self-rising flour

caramel sauce
½ cup (120 g) butter
¾ cup (170 g) light brown sugar
6 tbsp heavy cream
¼ cup (30 g) chopped pecans or
   almonds (optional)

Preheat the oven to 320°F (160°C). Grease a 7 x 9 in (18 x 23 cm) or 8 in (20 cm) square baking dish with butter.

In a large bowl, combine the dates and boiling water. Mix in the vanilla, cocoa powder, and baking soda and set aside to soak for about 30 minutes, or until the dates have soaked up most of the liquid.

Using an electric mixer or whisk, beat the butter and sugar together until pale and creamy. Add the beaten eggs and sift in the flour, continuing to stir until well combined. Fold the softened dates mixture into the batter. Pour into the prepared dish and smooth the top.

Bake for 40 minutes or until a knife inserted into the center comes out clean.

Meanwhile, make the sauce: In a medium saucepan set over medium–low heat, gently melt the butter, sugar, and cream together until the sugar has dissolved. Bring to a simmer, stirring constantly, then increase the heat until the mixture is boiling. Add the chopped nuts, if using, and remove from the heat.

Serve the cake in the dish, or cut into squares, spooning over the caramel sauce, and garnishing with a sprinkling of chopped nuts.

Chocolate & cardamom puddings

Serve this gorgeous rich dessert in small shot-glass size glasses. Freshly ground cardamom seeds will give the best flavor but you can use ground cardamom in a pinch.

❧ Serves 8   ❧ Prep time: 20 mins   ❧ Setting time: 4–6 hours

1¼ cups (300 ml) heavy cream
7 oz (200 g) dark chocolate, chopped
2–3 cardamom pods, seeds
   extracted and ground, or
   ⅛–¼ tsp ground cardamom
pinch of ground cinnamon
2 egg yolks
7 oz (200 g) mascarpone

to garnish
whipped cream
chopped pistachios
edible gold leaf (optional)

In a saucepan, gently heat the cream over medium heat just until it starts to simmer. Remove from the heat and add the chopped chocolate, whisking until it has melted.

Add the cardamom and cinnamon.

Whisk in egg yolks until incorporated, then whisk in the mascarpone until everything is well combined.

Divide among small glasses and chill in the refrigerator for 4–6 hours or until set.

Decorate with a spoonful of whipped cream, chopped pistachios, and edible gold leaf, if desired.

Kheeraj with rose petals & pistachios

Kheeraj is a traditional rice pudding, served often in Indian homes. You will come across different versions since all Indian families have their own way of making it. My recipe has simple flavors and is best served with homemade puris (page 158) and cream.

🦋 Serves 6–8   🦋 Prep time: 15 mins   🦋 Cooking time: 1 hour

1 cup (200 g) basmati rice, rinsed and soaked in cold water for 1 hour
1 tbsp ghee or butter
4 cups (1 liter) milk
4 cups (1 liter) water
⅔–1 cup condensed milk, to taste
¼ cup (40 g) raisins or golden raisins

to serve
pinch of saffron (optional)
chopped pistachio nuts
edible rose petals
scant 1 cup (200 ml) light cream

Rinse and drain the rice and place it in a large saucepan, along with the ghee or butter, milk, and water.

Bring to a boil, then reduce the heat to its lowest setting, cover, and simmer until all the liquid has been absorbed, about 1 hour.

Remove from the heat. If you would like a creamier pudding, use a handheld immersion blender to pureé the mixture, or leave it as it is. Add some condensed milk and taste, adding more if you like it sweeter. Return to the heat until heated through, stirring to ensure the mixture is well combined.

Stir through raisins, garnish with saffron, pistachios, and edible rose petals, if desired, and serve with cream for drizzling,

Zarina's burfi

Burfi is a delectable Indian sweet served at almost every special occasion. This is my mother's recipe and I have lots of fond memories of eating this creamy fudge-like treat at family gatherings.

❄ Makes 24–26 pieces ❄ Prep time: 20 mins ❄ Cooking time: 20 mins ❄ Setting time: 2–3 hours

4 cups (500 g) powdered
  whole milk
2 tbsp very soft ghee or butter
scant 1 cup (200 ml) heavy cream
½ cup (120 ml) water
1¼ cups (250 g) sugar

to garnish
chopped pistachios
edible rose petals
silver sugar pearls (optional)

In a large bowl, use your fingers to rub the powdered milk, ghee or butter, and the cream together until the mixture looks like fine breadcrumbs.

In a large pot, combine the water and sugar and simmer over medium heat for 8–10 minutes, until the sugar is completely dissolved and you have a thick, but runny syrup.

Remove from the heat and, using a wooden spoon, mix in the milk powder mixture, stirring until it comes together.

Line a 7 x 9 in (18 x 23 cm) or an 8 in (20 cm) square cake pan or baking dish with parchment paper and spread the mixture into the pan so it is about ½ in (1½ cm) thick.

Smooth the top and decorate with chopped pistachios, edible rose petals, and sugar pearls, if desired. Refrigerate for 2–3 hours to set.

Cut into small squares or rectangles and serve cold or at room temperature.

These will keep in an airtight container in the refrigerator for 1 week.

Cardamom shortbread cookies

I absolutely love homemade buttery melt-in-the-mouth shortbread cookies. This is a great recipe from my mother-in-law, but for a slightly Eastern twist I have added cardamom, and I decorate the shortbread with edible rose petals.

Makes 20—24   Prep time: 25 mins   Baking time: 18—20 mins

1 cup (250 g) butter, softened, plus
   extra for greasing
¾ cup (85 g) confectioner's sugar
½ cup (60 g) cornstarch
2 cups (240 g) all-purpose flour,
   plus extra for dusting
¼ tsp salt
3—4 cardamom pods, seeds
   extracted and ground

to garnish
½ cup (60 g) confectioner's sugar
2—3 cardamom pods, slightly
   crushed
8—10 dried edible rose petals,

In a large bowl, combine the butter and confectioner's sugar and, using a hand mixer or whisk, mix until pale and creamy.

Sift in the cornstarch, flour, salt, and cardamom into the butter and sugar and mix to combine.

Turn out onto a lightly floured surface and knead for about 5 minutes, pushing the mixture with your hands until it forms a smooth dough.

Roll the mixture into a log 2—2½ in (5—6 cm) thick, then wrap it in parchment paper and chill in the refrigerator for 10—15 minutes to firm up.

Preheat the oven to 320°F (160°C). Lightly grease 2 baking pans with butter and line with parchment paper.

Remove the dough from the refrigerator, remove the paper, and cut the roll into ½ in (1 cm) thick slices. Evenly space them on the prepared pans.

Bake the shortbread for 18—20 minutes, or until just colored. Set aside to cool. (If you are baking in batches, store unbaked dough in the refrigerator until ready to bake.)

In a bowl, combine the confectioner's sugar, cardamom, and dried rose petals and mix well. Use a sieve to dust the cooled shortbread.

Nimish

This rich, creamy pudding is made the night before to allow it to set. Serve it in little dishes as a refreshing dessert, with jalebi (page 189) on the side if you like.

❋ Serves 6–8　　❋ Prep time: 20 mins　　❋ Setting time: overnight

pinch of saffron threads
¼ cup (60 ml) warm milk
scant 2 cups (450 ml) heavy cream
1½–2 tbsp confectioner's sugar,
　sifted
1 tsp rosewater

to garnish (optional)
rose petals
edible silver leaf
chopped nuts

In a small bowl, soak the saffron threads in the warm milk for 10 minutes. Leave to cool.

Pour the cream into a large bowl. Using a hand mixer or whisk, whip the cream just until you start getting soft peaks—it's really important not to over-whip.

Add the confectioner's sugar, rosewater, and the cooled saffron milk. Whisk for a further minute or so until it is all combined.

Pour into glasses or small dessert bowls, cover, and chill overnight.

Decorate with your preferred garnishes and serve chilled.

Jalebi

These fried batter coils coated in sugar syrup are a traditional Indian sweet, and a hot favorite at festive celebrations such as birthdays and holidays. The saffron is optional, but adds authenticity and a depth of flavor. These are ideal with the cold nimish (page 187)

❋ Makes approx. 18–20 coils ❋ Prep time: 20 mins ❋ Cooking time: 25–30 mins

2 cups (250 g) all-purpose flour
1½ tbsp fine semolina
½ tsp baking powder
good pinch of salt
2 tbsp plain yogurt
1⅔–2 cups (400–500 ml) water
pinch of saffron threads (optional)
2 drops of orange food coloring
vegetable oil, for deep-frying

syrup
1¼ cups (300 ml) water
1¼ cups (250 g) sugar
¼ tsp saffron threads (optional)
2 tsp orange food coloring
¼ tsp rosewater

First, make the batter: In a large bowl, combine the flour, semolina, baking powder, salt, and yogurt. Gradually mix in enough of the water to make a thick but pourable batter. Add the saffron, if desired, and food coloring. Mix and set aside for 20–30 minutes.

For the syrup: combine the water and sugar in a saucepan and stir over low–medium heat until the sugar has dissolved. Add the saffron, food coloring, and rosewater and simmer for 10–15 minutes until it has reduced to a syrup.

To fry the coils: pour the oil into a deep pot or small karahi (Indian wok) to a depth of 2 in (5 cm). Heat until the surface shimmers and a small piece of bread turns golden.

Whisk the rested batter and transfer to a squeezy bottle with a nozzle.

Working in batches of 2–3 at a time, squeeze batter into the hot oil in little coils and fry for about 40 seconds, turning so they become crisp and golden on all sides

Transfer to a plate lined with paper towels to drain excess oil.

Immerse the coils in the hot syrup to coat both sides, letting the excess syrup drip off, and serve immediately.

Creamy halva

Very similar to Italian panna cotta, halva is a delicious, creamy Indian dessert that is easy to make and a lovely cooling way to finish your Indian meal. It needs a few hours to set in the fridge.

🐝 Serves 4–6 🐝 Prep time: 15 mins 🐝 Cooking time: 15 mins 🐝 Setting time: 3–4 hours

1¼ cups (300 ml) light cream
2 cups (500 ml) milk
¼ cup (50 g) sugar
1 tsp agar-agar, mixed with
   1 tbsp of water
2 tsp semolina
1 tsp vanilla extrac
a few saffron threads (optional)

to garnish
chopped nuts
a few saffron threads (optional)

In a bowl, whisk the cream and milk together until well combined. Pour into a saucepan, add the sugar, and bring to a boil.

Reduce the heat to a simmer and stir in the agar agar mixture, semolina, vanilla extract, and a few saffron threads, if desired. Simmer for 7 minutes, stirring occasionally.

Pour into a shallow dish or dessert glasses and set aside to cool for 30 minutes or so, until just beginning to set. Sprinkle with chopped nuts and saffron and refrigerate until cold and firm, 3–4 hours. Serve cold.

Şakar para

Sakar para are delicious diamond-cut, deep-fried pastry cookies. This recipe is for a sweet, sugar-coated version that is ideal for an afternoon tea with guests. Mom used to make them during school vacations, and we would help her cut them into diamond shapes. They are best fried as soon as you have made the dough, and eaten on the same day.

🌿 Makes 30–40 pieces   🌿 Prep time: 20 mins   🌿 Cooking time: 30 mins

1 cup (250 ml) milk
1 cup (200 g) sugar
4 cups (500 g) all-purpose flour,
  plus extra for dusting
½ cup (120 g) ghee or butter,
  softened
vegetable oil, for frying
confectioner's sugar, for dusting

In a saucepan, combine the milk and sugar and bring to a boil. Simmer vigorously until the sugar dissolves, about 5 minutes. Remove from the heat and set aside to cool.

Sift the flour into a large bowl and then add the ghee or butter. Using your fingers, rub it in until the mixture is well combined. Add the cooled milk mixture and mix until it forms a dough.

Turn out onto a lightly floured surface and roll the dough out to a thickness of around ⅛ in (5 mm).

Pour the oil into a large pot to a depth of 2 in (5 cm). Heat until the surface shimmers and a small piece of bread turns golden.

Meanwhile, cut the dough into diamond shapes about 2 in (5 cm) in length. Working in batches, fry the diamonds for 2–3 minutes, turning them so they are crisp and evenly golden on both sides.

Transfer to a plate lined with paper towels to drain excess oil.

Once cool, dust with confectioner's sugar and serve.

Jeero snacks

This is another one of those lovely afternoon-tea snacks I grew up eating. It is more of a savory cookie, with a little hint of spice from the jeero (cumin).

❀ Makes approx. 30–40 pieces　　❀ Prep time: 20 mins　　❀ Cooking time: 30 mins

2 cups (240 g) all-purpose flour,
　plus extra for dusting
1 tsp baking powder
4 tbsp (60 g) ghee or butter,
　softened
1 tbsp lemon juice
1 tsp cumin seeds, crushed
¼ cup (60 ml) cold milk
vegetable oil, for frying

to garnish
pinch of salt
whole cumin seeds

In a large bowl, sift the flour and baking powder together. Using your fingers, rub in the butter and lemon juice until the mixture resembles fine breadcrumbs.

Mix in the crushed cumin seeds, and just enough of the cold milk to form a soft dough.

Turn out onto a lightly floured work surface and roll the dough out until it is about the thickness of a tortilla or roti. Cut into thin strips.

Pour the oil into a large pot to a depth of 2 in (5 cm). Heat until the surface shimmers and a small piece of bread turns golden. Working in batches, fry the strips for 2–3 minutes, turning them so they are crisp and evenly golden on both sides.

Transfer to a plate lined with paper towels to drain excess oil. Sprinkle with salt and whole cumin seeds and serve.

Gulab jamun

Gulab jamun means "rose plum." It is a very popular Indian sweet, which is actually fried balls of dough soaked in syrup—a little like doughnuts. My friends and family just love them. I like to serve them with mascarpone or whipped cream to cut through the sweetness.

❋ Makes 18–20   ❋ Prep time: 30 mins   ❋ Cooking time: 30 mins

syrup
2 cups (400 g) sugar
4 cups (1 liter) water
4–6 drops of rosewater

gulab jamun
scant 1 cup (100 g) powdered milk
2 tbsp self-rising flour
2 tsp fine semolina
2 tbsp ghee or butter
4 tbsp milk
vegetable oil, for frying

edible rose petals, to garnish
  (optional)
mascarpone or whipped cream,
  to serve (optional)

For the syrup, combine the sugar and water in a large heavy-based saucepan. Stir over low heat until the sugar dissolves. Bring to a boil, add the rosewater, and remove from the heat. Leave aside to cool.

To make the gulab jamun: In a large bowl, mix the powdered milk, flour, semolina, and ghee or butter until combined. Mix in just enough of the milk to make a soft, smooth dough.

Using your hands, roll the dough into 18–20 small balls, 1½–2 in (5–6 cm) in diameter.

Pour the oil into a karahi (Indian wok) or large pot to a depth of 2 in (5 cm); it should be no more than one-third full. Heat until the surface shimmers and a small piece of bread turns golden. Working in batches, fry the balls for 3–4 minutes, turning frequently, until dark golden all over. (Watch carefully—this can happen quickly.)

Using a slotted spoon, transfer them directly to the syrup. When all the balls have been added to the syrup, return the syrup to a boil, then remove from the heat. Use a slotted spoon to transfer the gulab jamun to a serving dish. Pour the remaining syrup into a small jug.

Decorate with rose petals, if desired, and serve at room temperature with a dollop of mascarpone or whipped cream, and extra syrup on the side.

Mango & saffron kulfi

I love recipes that encourage you to try flavors and spices you might not usually use. This is a simple kulfi (Indian ice cream) recipe that's ideal for summer entertaining, and it only takes minutes to prepare. I've included my favorite flavor, but there are many combinations you can try. Mango pulp is available at any Indian grocery store, or you can use fresh mango purée.

❋ Serves 6　　　　　❋ Prep time: 20 mins　　　　❋ Freezing time 4–6 hours

2½ cups (600 ml) heavy cream
1¼ cups (300 ml) condensed milk
½ cup (120 ml) mango pulp
　(fresh, frozen, or canned)
pinch of saffron
3–4 cardamom pods, seeds
　extracted and ground
saffron threads, to garnish
6 waffle cones (optional)

Using an electric mixer, whisk the cream just until it starts to thicken. Slowly add the condensed milk and whip to soft peaks.

Add the mango pulp, saffron, and cardamom and continue to whip until you have stiff peaks.

Pour into a cake pan or plastic tub, sprinkle with saffron threads, cover well, and freeze overnight for best results, or for at least 4–6 hours if you want to serve it sooner.

Serve in bowls or waffle cones.

Pavlova with rose cream, cardamom & salted caramel shards

The first time I had pavlova was when I was invited to a Christmas lunch with my husband's family. This is my mother-in-law, Wendy's recipe, to which I have added an Eastern twist.

❀ Serves 8–10   ❀ Prep time: 30 mins   ❀ Baking time: 1½ hours

meringue base
4 egg whites
3 tbsp cold water
1 cup (200 g) sugar
1 tbsp cornstarch
1 tsp vanilla extract
1 tsp white vinegar

rose cream
1¼ cups (300 ml) heavy cream
2 drops of rosewater

salted caramel shards
1 cup (200 g) sugar
¼ cup (60 ml) water
1–2 cardamom pods, seeds
  extracted and crushed
1 tbsp sea salt flakes

topping
1 cup (240 g) fresh berries of
  your choice, or a mixture of
  pomegranate seeds, chopped nuts,
  and edible rose petals

Preheat the oven to 320°F (160°C). Grease a large sheet of foil, then run it under cold water and use it to line a large baking pan.

In a very clean bowl or stand mixer, beat the egg whites to stiff peaks. Add the water, then gradually beat in the sugar. Slow the beater and add the cornstarch. Next add the vanilla and vinegar. The mixture should now be stiff and glossy and should stay in whichever position you pull it. Using a flat spatula, pile the mixture onto the foil-lined baking pan in a circular mound about 4 in (10 cm) high and 9 in (23 cm) in diameter, gently flattening the top so you can decorate it. Then, working from the base, use light upward strokes to create swirls.

Bake for 15 minutes, then turn the temperature down to 220°F (105°C) and continue to bake for 1 hour, until the meringue is a light creamy color and pulls off the baking sheet easily. Turn off the heat and leave in the oven to cool completely (it can be left overnight).

Meanwhile, make the rose cream: In a large bowl or mixer, whip the cream with the rosewater until soft peaks form, being careful not to over-whip. Set aside.

To make the shards, line a baking pan with a sheet of foil. Combine the sugar and water in a saucepan over low heat. Add the cardamom seeds and cook, stirring continuously, until all of the sugar has dissolved. Increase the heat to high and simmer for 4–5 minutes, swirling the pan occasionally and brushing down the sides with a damp pastry brush, until you have a light golden caramel. Carefully pour this onto the prepared pan, swirling and tilting to spread the caramel. Sprinkle with the salt. Cool in the refrigerator until hard, then break into shards. (This can be prepared up to a day ahead and stored in an airtight container.)

Once the meringue is cool, decorate it with the rose-infused cream, toppings of your choice, and salted caramel shards.

Cardamom cake with mascarpone & rose icing

This beautiful cake is dense and moist, and full of Eastern flavors I love: rose, cardamom, and pistachios. Serve as a delicious accompaniment to afternoon tea.

❀ Serves 10   ❀ Prep time: 15 mins   ❀ Baking time: 35 mins

13 tbsp (200 g) butter, softened,
   plus extra for greasing
3 eggs, whisked
1¼ cups (75 g) condensed milk
1 tbsp rosewater
2 cups (250 g) self-rising flour,
   sifted
1 tsp baking powder
1 tsp ground cardamom

icing
9 oz (250 g) mascarpone
2 tbsp confectioner's sugar, sifted
1–2 tsp rosewater

to garnish
¼ cup (30 g) pistachios, some
   crushed

Preheat the oven to 320°F (160°C). Grease a 10 in (25 cm) round cake pan with butter.

In a large bowl, use an electric mixer or whisk to beat the butter until creamy and then mix in the eggs, condensed milk, and rosewater.

Add the flour, baking powder, and cardamom. Gently mix just until combined, but don't over-mix.

Pour the batter into the prepared pan and bake for 35 minutes or until a skewer inserted into the center comes out clean. Let it cool before turning it out.

Meanwhile, prepare the icing: In a large bowl or stand mixer, beat together the mascarpone, confectioner's sugar, and rosewater until it is of a spreadable consistency.

Using a spatula, spread the icing on top of the cake. Decorate with crushed and whole pistachios.

Frosted berry & chai loaf

The chai flavors work beautifully in this berry loaf and the color of the icing makes it a stunning dessert for a special occasion. I have used raspberries for this recipe but blueberries work well, too.

❋ Serves 10   ❋ Prep time: 15 mins   ❋ Baking time: 45 mins

⅔ cup (150 ml) milk
2 chai-flavored tea bags
2 eggs
1 cup (200 g) sugar
½ tsp vanilla extract
1⅔ cups (200 g) all-purpose flour
1 tsp baking powder
1 tsp ground cinnamon
5 tbsp vegetable oil
1 cup (120 g) fresh raspberries

icing
2 cups (225 g) confectioner's
  sugar, sifted
¼ cup (60 g) fresh or partly
  thawed raspberries

to garnish
¼ cup (60 g) fresh raspberries
edible flowers

Preheat the oven to 340°F (170°C). Grease and line a 9½ by 4 in (24 x 10 cm) loaf pan with parchment paper.

In a small saucepan, bring the milk to a boil and add the tea bags. Stir, then remove from the heat and set aside to steep and cool.

In a large bowl, use an electric mixer to beat the eggs, sugar, and vanilla together, until thick and glossy.

Sift in the flour, baking powder, and cinnamon and gently mix. Add the oil and a scant ½ cup (100 ml) of the milk tea (the teabags will have absorbed some of the milk, so you will have to squeeze them to end up with the right amount). Mix at a slow speed just until fully combined, being careful not to over-mix.

In a separate bowl, crush the berries with a fork, retaining some of the shape, and don't worry too much about the juice as this is what you want laced through the cake. Gently fold through the cake mixture.

Pour the mixture into the prepared pan and bake for 45 minutes, or until a skewer comes out clean. Cool completely before turning out.

Meanwhile, make the icing: In a blender, mix the confectioner's sugar and berries together until you have a thick, spreadable paste.

Using a knife, spread the icing over the loaf. Decorate with fresh berries and edible flowers.

Graham's orange slices with orange blossom icing

My mother-in-law made these slices for me when I came home from the hospital after having our son, and I've loved these slices ever since. It's also a childhood favorite of my husband's and he will often whip up a batch when we have an urge for something sweet.

❦ Serves 6–8   ❦ Prep time: 20–30 mins

9 tbsp (125 g) butter
3 tbsp condensed milk
zest of 1 orange
9 oz (250 g) rich tea cookies,
   finely crushed
½ cup (30 g) unsweetened
   shredded coconut

icing
2–3 tbsp orange juice, strained
   and warmed
2 drops of orange blossom water
1 cup (110 g) confectioner's
   sugar, sifted

to garnish
strips of orange zest

In a saucepan, melt the butter and condensed milk together over low heat, stirring until smooth. Do not allow it to boil.

In a bowl, combine the orange zest, crushed cookies, and coconut. Pour it into the butter mixture, and mix well. You will find it combines easily.

Press the mixture into a 13 x 9 in (32 x 23 cm) jelly-roll pan and refrigerate for 15 minutes or so to cool.

Once cooled, prepare the icing. In a bowl, mix the warmed orange juice, orange blossom water, and confectioner's sugar until smooth and the mixture coats the back of the spoon. Spread evenly over the cookie base in the pan.

Place the pan back in the refrigerator until the icing is firm. Cut into slices and decorate with orange zest.

Store leftovers in an airtight container in the refrigerator.

Almond & pistachio ladoo

These soft, fudgy Indian bliss balls melt in your mouth and taste divine. I love this simple recipe, given to me by my dear friend Shweta. They are just the right size for an after-dinner treat.

❀ Makes approx. 15   ❀ Prep time: 30—40 mins

1¼ cups (300 ml) ghee or butter
½ cup (40 g) chickpea (gram) flour
1 cup (115 g) wholewheat flour
½ cup (80 g) coarse semolina
1¼ cups (100 g) almond meal
1 cup (200 g) sugar
¼ cup (30 g) chopped nuts or pitted
   and chopped dates (optional)
unsweetened shredded coconut or
   finely chopped nuts, for rolling
   (optional)

In a large pot, gently heat the ghee or butter over medium heat until it has melted.

Add the gram flour, stirring with a wooden spoon, and then the other flours. Cook, stirring constantly, for 10–15 minutes until the mixture is soft and pliable. It does take a little while, so take your time and make sure it doesn't catch.

Mix in the almond meal, followed by the sugar, and chopped nuts or finely chopped dates if you're using them. Cook, stirring, for 10–15 minutes more until the mixture has turned a lovely golden color. (It is important to make sure this also doesn't catch or it will smell and taste burnt.)

Remove from the heat and set aside until cool enough to handle. Using clean hands, roll the mixture into small bite-sized balls. If you wish you can roll them in shredded coconut or finely chopped nuts.

Alternatively, instead of rolling the mixture into balls, my mother spreads it onto a baking pan while still warm and, once cooled, cuts it into slices.

Masala chaa

Chaa or chai are the Indian words for tea: it doesn't refer to the flavor; the spices or "masala" that go into the tea give it the flavor. This easy-to-make chaa is delicious on its own or served with sakar para (page 193).

❋ Makes 2 cups   ❋ Prep time: 10 mins

1 cup (250 ml) water
1 cup (250 ml) milk
1 tbsp sugar
2 in (5 cm) cinnamon stick
3 cloves
3 whole cardamom pods
3–4 English breakfast teabags,
   depending on how strong you
   like your tea.

Combine all the ingredients in a saucepan and bring to a boil.

Reduce the heat and simmer for 3–4 minutes, until fragrant.

Strain and pour into glasses or cups and serve hot.

Hyder kheer

While turmeric lattes have become a very popular in recent years, my mom has been making hyder kheer since I was a child. Turmeric has many healing properties, and we used to drink this at the first sign of a cold.

❋ Makes 2 cups   ❋ Prep time: 10 mins   ❋ Cooking time: 3–5 mins

2 cups (500 ml) milk
¾ tsp turmeric
¼ tsp cinnamon
pinch of saffron (optional)
1 tsp honey

to garnish
additional cinnamon or saffron

Place the milk in a saucepan and start to heat gently.

Add the turmeric, cinnamon, a pinch of saffron (if using), and the honey and heat just until it starts boiling.

If you have a milk frother, you can froth some of the turmeric milk if you wish and pour it on top.

Pour into mugs and sprinkle with cinnamon or saffron.

Lassi

Conceivably the world's oldest version of the smoothie, this creamy, yogurt-based drink is fantastic for cooling you down in hot weather. Equally it's a great accompaniment to a spicy curry and helps with digestion. Our favorite family flavors are mango, salt, or rose lassi, but if you wanted to experiment, there are lots of combinations you could try.

❋ Each recipe serves 2   ❋ Prep time: 15 mins

mango lassi
1 lb (500 g) mango pulp
   (fresh, frozen, or canned)
1 cup (250 ml) chilled milk
1 cup (250 ml) plain yogurt
small handful ice cubes
honey or maple syrup, if needed
handful of chopped pistachios, to
   garnish (optional)

salt lassi
½ tsp sea salt flakes
1⅔ cups (400 ml) plain yogurt
scant 1 cup (200 ml) water
small handful ice cubes
1 tsp toasted cumin seeds,
   to garnish

rose lassi
2–3 tsp rosewater
1 drop red food coloring
   (or less, depending on how pink
   you want the color)
1 cup (250 ml) chilled milk
1 cup (250 ml) plain yogurt
small handful ice cubes
pomegranate seeds, to garnish

For each lassi, blend all of the ingredients (except for the garnish) together in a blender until smooth.

Pour into glasses, sprinkle the garnish on top, and serve chilled.

Acknowledgments

There are many people to whom I am exceptionally grateful for helping me realize my long-held dream of writing my own cookbook. I would like to especially thank the following:

The team at Potton & Burton, in particular Emma Radcliffe, who saw my vision, and has been an amazing sounding board, prop-finder extraordinaire, and a wonderful support throughout this process.

Manja Wachsmuth for the beautiful photographic representation of my recipes, Bernadette Hogg, for the food styling of the lifestyle photography, Lauren Culpan and Lucy Parker for their help on the shoot days. Thanks also to my amazing Kickstarter supporters who helped fund the photography.

Charlotte King, without whose help in looking after Zara and our dog, Holly, I would not have survived the summer holidays cooking, writing, and photographing.

Thanks to Anne from Founders of Rome, Takapuna, for the gorgeous copper props; to Simon Feast at Westlake Boys High School for the fantastic wooden boards found in the school sheds, which have featured as backdrops in many of the photos and to Early Settler in Wairau Road, Auckland.

Thanks to my wonderful friends Mandy, Ian, and Jess Curry, Arnaz Mehta, and Michelle and Greg Johansson for their support and being there when I needed them.

And finally, my lovely family—my parents Hamid and Zarina, for their never-ending love, support, and encouragement. My three beautiful sisters, Anjum, Farha, and Nishat, who always try my recipes, share my love of cooking, and are the best food critics.

A heartfelt thank you to my best friend and life partner, Graham. Without his support and love, I couldn't have done this.

Lastly, to Adam and Zara, my beautiful children: "Let the beauty of what you love be what you do." I hope you love cooking as much as I do.

Many thanks,

Ashia

Index